HOW CHILDREN SUCCEED

12 STEPS TO HELP PREPARE YOUR KIDS FOR SUCCESS

HOW CHILDREN SUCCEED

12 STEPS TO HELP PREPARE YOUR KIDS FOR SUCCESS

RACHEL BURGESS

Rachel Burgess © Copyright 2019

All rights reserved.

The content contained within this book may not be reproduced, duplicated or transmitted without direct written permission from the author or the publisher.

Under no circumstances will any blame or legal responsibility be held against the publisher, or author, for any damages, reparation, or monetary loss due to the information contained within this book, either directly or indirectly.

Legal Notice:

This book is copyright protected. It is only for personal use. You cannot amend, distribute, sell, use, quote or paraphrase any part, or the content within this book, without the consent of the author or publisher.

Disclaimer Notice:

Please note the information contained within this document is for educational and entertainment purposes only. All effort has been executed to present accurate, up to date, reliable, complete information. No warranties of any kind are declared or implied. Readers acknowledge that the author is not engaging in the rendering of legal, financial, medical or professional advice. The content within this book has been derived from various sources. Please consult a licensed professional before attempting any techniques outlined in this book.

By reading this document, the reader agrees that under no circumstances is the author responsible for any losses, direct or indirect, that are incurred as a result of the use of information contained within this document, including, but not limited to, errors, omissions, or inaccuracies.

TABLE OF CONTENTS

Introduction .... *iii*

   Benefits of the Book vi

Chapter 1 .... *1*

   Benefits of Chores 2
      Starting the Routine 8

Chapter 2 .... *15*

   Failing Is Not Failure 16
      The Emotional Response 25

Chapter 3 .... *31*

   Benefits of Learning Basic Skills 32
      How to Help 38

Chapter 4 .... *45*

   Benefits of High Expectations 46
      How to Hold Expectations 52

Chapter 5 .... *57*

   The Right Mindset 58
      Praise in Action 63

Chapter 6 .... *71*

   Creating Healthy Relationships 72
      Fostering Social Skills 81

Chapter 7 .... *87*

   The Importance of Physical Health 88

How to Promote Healthy Choices..94

Chapter 8 101

Catching Feelings 102
Keeping Happy...107

Chapter 9 115

Why It's Important 116
How to Teach Them..122

Chapter 10 129

What They Can Learn 130
How to Raise an Entrepreneur 133

Chapter 11 143

Physical Activity 144
Establishing Confidence...149

Chapter 12 157

What to Look For 158
Teaching Social Skills 165

Conclusion 171

References 177

YOUR FREE GIFT

As a way to saying thank you for your purchase, I have included a gift in this book that shows tips about ways to handle various types of behaviors with children. I know that when dealing with kids, you always need extra tips. These are more lessons that I learned and wasn't able to categorize in the book, therefore I made it as a pamphlet as a gift for you getting this book. You can find it at rachelburgessbooks.com. Enjoy!

How Children Succeed

INTRODUCTION

Every parent wants their child to be successful; it's human nature. So we spend hours holding the back of their bike seat until they can pedal on their own, we sit with them while they do homework, and we try to keep our cool during every tantrum. Sometimes, every mother feels unqualified for the job that life has given her, but I'm here to pull back the curtain and share the secrets of parenting.

There are tons of parenting techniques and strategies available to us today, but only a few are guaranteed to foster the most important life skills in your children. That's why I've taken the time to pick them out of the thousands of other options and compile them in an easy-to-read format. The strategies are so simple, you won't have to think twice about implementing them in your life.

How Children Succeed

Sounds too good to be true? It's not, but it takes hard work. The key is to implement these strategies now so your child can develop the skills as early as possible. Toddlers are the best age to create healthy habits because they love to make you happy (despite having a meltdown every time you go to the grocery store). If you can teach your toddler the basic foundations of skills such as responsibility, emotional intelligence, and helping, then you have laid the groundwork for a successful adult.

This book will give you the tools to make your dreams a reality. We've all been through the parenting books with vague suggestions and lackluster descriptions, so I've made sure to walk you through multiple ways of achieving each step. Every child is different and sometimes this means trying the same strategy four different ways until you find the technique that sticks.

Some things you can start with your children when they are young include reading, math, chores, and friendships with others. There are a variety of ways you can approach these activities, so your child is sure to find them fun and engaging. When you implement these habits, it might be difficult to know where your expectations for success should fall. The answer: shoot for the stars! Kids rise to their parents' expectations, so don't be afraid to challenge your child.

As a mother of three, I want to make sure my children have all the tools they will need to succeed as adults. It's hard to know if you are doing the right things as a parent, especially when your child is screaming and resisting your rules, but these techniques have worked so well with my family that I feel much more confident as a mother.

When I started talking to my friends about the rules and procedures I have set up for my kids and my parenting style, I realized that most of them felt just as lost and alone as I did before I found these techniques. The adage, "It takes a village," has stayed around this long for a reason. They needed help, so I decided to step in. I wrote this book to help other parents feel equipped to raise competent adults and have confidence in their strategies. You will be able to watch your children soar to heights you've never imagined and know that it was because of your dedication to their success.

Benefits of the Book

When you implement activities and rules that focus on developing your child mentally, physically, and emotionally, you will be amazed at the results. You will notice your child taking initiative around the house, helping you and their siblings, and maybe even telling you how to help like my three-year-old does. I remember the first time I saw my oldest child doing chores; I thought I was dreaming. The living room was too quiet, so I popped my head in to make sure he was okay to find him pulling clean clothes from the basket I left on the floor and "folding" them. I asked him what he was doing, and he replied, "Helping."

It's moments like this where you realize that giving your child these opportunities for growth can benefit you, too. When your children pitch in around the house, you will probably feel happier and less stressed, which can free up time to have fun with them.

The parenting strategies I use and will teach you about are used by tons of families because they work. If you asked a friend how they managed such a well-behaved child, they will probably cite one or more of the most common methods such as praising positive behavior. After discussing strategies such as this one with friends, I had people constantly coming back to thank me for the tip. After some time and practice, their children were acting more conscientiously and handle their emotions more effectively. One friend even said, "She's like a whole new kid!"

I know that, personally, by creating a more constructive environment for my children, I have been able to have a better relationship with them. We now sit around the living room and do laundry together, we eat a healthy dinner together every night, and we take family walks around the neighborhood. I feel so much more in touch with my children than ever before and it's a feeling I wouldn't trade for the world.

You probably picked up this book because you want that same feeling. You want to know that your child can rely on you and they are also developing into the best person they can be. I can assure you, that you've come to the right place. Here, you will learn everything you need to know about how to raise competent children who can become prosperous adults.

Each chapter focuses on a specific strategy you can use to instill certain skills in your child. I include an array of suggestions on how to implement these and important notes about how your behavior surrounding the task will affect your child. As a parent, it's easy to say one thing and do another, but we have to remember that our children are watching our actions more than they are listening to our words. If we can set a good example, then they will be sure to follow in our footsteps.

The earlier you can start cementing these skills, the better. Using your toddler's energy and desire to please can be much easier than fighting a teenager's habits and desire to be independent. The younger your child is, the longer they have to develop these skills and apply them to their lives. It might seem strange to ask your two or three-year-old to do chores, but remember that they see it all as time spent with you.

If you have an older child, don't panic. You can still use the tools I'm talking about. You'll just need to modify your approach. Lucky for you, I've included ways to help children of all ages get into these new routines. So whether you're expecting a baby, surviving with your young child, or worried about your teenager's future, starting my strategies immediately will be the best way to get them on the right track.

CHAPTER 1

Make Them Do Chores

Odds are you grew up doing chores. Most people did, but this is a waning commonality among modern families. What caused this shift? Perhaps it's the tiresome and unrelenting duty of disciplining children winning out, or people's reluctance to follow in their parents' footsteps. Whatever the reason, refraining from requiring your children do chores can do them more harm than good.

Chores can help kids develop better judgement, teach them how to control their impulses, and show them how to be more empathetic toward others. If you allow your child to help around the house, they will determine which tasks need to be completed. They also learn that they cannot do the things they want to do immediately because there are responsibilities to finish first. This shows them that to do the fun things in life, they also have to do the work. Finally, if you frame chores as a helping activity, it will teach your child to look for opportunities to assist others.

Benefits of Chores

For some parents, putting your child to work can seem strange. You want to allow them to enjoy their time as a kid and you know how hard they work at school and in their extracurricular activities. Putting them to work as soon as they walk through the door might feel mean or unfair. You might even think your child doesn't have the time to do any chores. Kids have such busy schedules these days, they might leave the house at 6 a.m. for school and not return home until 6 p.m. after soccer practice. Where are you supposed to stick in chores when they still have to eat, bathe, and do homework?

Despite seeming impossibilities, requiring chores from your kids is not an unreasonable request. Besides making your life a little easier, giving your children tasks around the house can benefit their overall development and success. It can give your kids the skills they need to be happy and independent individuals.

This is because doing chores can make a child feel like they are capable of doing things adults do—and what does any child want more than to be like their parents? When they complete household tasks, they know that they are helping their parents and that they can do things for themselves. This can foster independence and confidence that will show in other areas of their lives, too.

Prioritizing chores along with copious amounts of homework and time spent at sports or band practices can instill an imperative lesson. It might seem like your child is always working, but you are also teaching them to diversify their skills. This can be helpful if they fail in one area and haven't put all their self-worth in one talent. Your child might lose a baseball game, but he knows he's still good in school and helpful at home.

Holding children accountable for completing their chores can teach them an important lesson in responsibility. When they understand that there are consequences to their actions, both good and bad, they will act in a more responsible way. This skill can follow them into adulthood and help them make important decisions about job opportunities or how they spend their free time.

Helping with tasks such as taking out the garbage or washing the dishes can develop basic life skills for children to fall back on when they finally move out of your home and into their own place. If they have been practicing basic tasks with you their entire lives, then washing their own clothes and keeping the kitchen clean will not seem as intimidating once they have to do it alone.

For younger children, these tasks might be too much to do on their own, but you can foster independence by considering their skill level. Letting them button their own shirts for school or put on their own shoes can help them feel like they are capable and talented. It can also eliminate the possibility of your child becoming upset when all their friends can do things such as tie their shoes and your kid doesn't know how.

As you surely know, not all chores are great for all age groups. You probably wouldn't leave your two-year-old to put dirty clothes in the washer and start the machine on their own, but your seven-year-old would be able to. It is important to consider your child's age and abilities to ensure their chore is something they can handle on their own.

How Children Succeed

Even if you think they're too young, preschool children are more than capable of doing chores around the house. As previously mentioned, it won't be anything complex, but they can learn to pick up their toys or clean up in their room. If you find your child needs extra motivation to do these tasks, you can use a sticker chart as a reward, but most small children enjoy helping their parents and won't need a reward system.

When your child is older and they start kindergarten, you can explain that as they grow up, they get to help out more around the house. There are a multitude of ways to frame this discussion, and you will know the best approach for your child.

As you increase responsibilities, the key is to add tasks instead of replacing older ones. If they could pick up toys and clothes in their room when they were four, then they can still pick them up when they are five. Try to build on the chores they are accustomed to by adding an extra step, such as cleaning their room and making their bed. This can help them to integrate new tasks into their routine.

The older your children get, the more complex their chores should be become. They can put away their own clean clothes or unload the dishwasher. As you introduce these new tasks, make sure to show your child the correct steps and encourage them through the process during their first couple of tries. It is important to remember that your child won't complete tasks perfectly the first time, and even though it might be slower going than if you did it yourself, taking the time to let them try is imperative to their success.

Once your child makes it to their tween years, they can take on significantly more responsibility and will not need as much encouragement or rewards. For this age group, cleaning tasks such as sweeping, mopping, or cleaning the bathroom are good options. These can be things they are expected to do every day or once a week, however you see fit for the needs of the household.

At this age, you can introduce an allowance if you would like, as this is when kids typically start seeing friends at places like the movies or the mall. If you aren't quite ready to give an allowance, you can create a token system where they work for things such as an extra hour of screen time or a sleepover with their friends.

Teenagers need to develop more practical skills that will help them in the real world. Chores such as mowing the grass, cooking meals, and washing the laundry can help them develop the basic life skills they will need to survive on their own. Allowance can be a great way to motivate a teenager, but should be on a predetermined schedule, just like getting a paycheck. This helps them practice budgeting and understanding the value of their money.

Starting the Routine

Let's face it: kids don't want to do chores. You don't have to bribe and bargain your way through an argument, though. Sometimes the key is simply to make sure they know you *expect* their help. An explanation of why they need to do a chore won't be necessary if your child understands that they are part of a family that works together.

Harnessing the energy of your toddler can be the perfect way to establish this mindset. Children want to be just like adults, so using that desire paired with their energy to encourage doing chores is a great way to train your child to be helpful. Let your toddler watch or help you with the chores you're doing around the house, even if it means making a bigger mess than you started with. It can show them that being part of a group means pitching in and helping others.

As they get older and you introduce new tasks, make sure you are encouraging the effort they put into the task. They won't be able to complete the chores perfectly—clothes might be in the wrong drawers or water might cover your countertops—but showing that you appreciate their effort will

How Children Succeed

make them want to continue helping and reinforce the habit.

Tweens can be difficult to manage and typically hate being directed by their parents, so try to find chores you don't have to ask them to do. If you instilled the ideas when they were young, they will see the full sink and know to wash the dishes. If you can teach them to look for ways to help instead of insisting they do specific chores, you might be more successful at generating participation.

Even though you might still see them as the baby you cared for so diligently, teenagers are basically miniature adults and should be treated as such. You can expect your teenager to complete any task that you can, and these should make up their usual routine. They can help with more difficult and time-consuming chores, such as building a piece of furniture or setting up a new piece of technology.

When you enforce chores, you might feel like you are constantly reminding your children to pick up, clean up, or wash up. It can be tiring to always threaten consequences and follow up with unfinished tasks, but do not give up. If you do the chores to save time or energy, it teaches your child that if they resist long enough someone else will handle their responsibilities.

You might even feel guilty about asking your children to do chores. In these situations, think about how important it is for children to follow a routine. Once they incorporate their daily tasks into this routine, they will complete their chores without you having to ask. You just have to get them there.

It might be difficult to believe that your four-year-old can do chores, but they are! Underestimating your child can lead to them underestimating themselves and being afraid to try new or scary things. If you aren't sure that your child is capable of a task, sit with them while they try it. Encourage them until they make it through to the end and you should be able to gauge if it was too difficult to ask them to do every day.

Sometimes even the word "chore" can present a problem. The word has developed such a negative connotation in our world, that when kids hear it, they immediately associate the task with a negative experience. You have the power to change their mindset by choosing the words you use. If you refer to tasks as helping, your child might be more inclined to complete them. For example, instead of asking, "Did you do your chores," you can ask, "Did you help me by folding the towels?"

Sometimes, no matter how you phrase it, your children are going to fight you to do chores. In these instances, we need to find ways to use our children's energy to work with us instead of against us.

This can all come down to how we treat our toddlers. A lot of us dread the "terrible twos," but it's actually the best age to start training helping children. At this age, you can start to encourage your child to do chores with you, such as washing dishes, folding laundry, or sweeping the living room. They might make more of a mess than you started with, but if you can remain calm and patient, your child will learn that helping with chores makes you happy.

It also empowers our children to know that they can do any task they want in the house. This mindset will stick with them as they grow up, too. So next time you're rushing to get chores done and your two-year-old asks what you're doing, let them help. Don't send them away to play with their toys so you can move faster. Encourage their helping spirit and put that energy to good use.

When you're working with children it is also imperative to make a habit stick. When your two-year-old wanders up to you to see what you're doing, it's because they want to do it with you. So when you give them tasks to complete, don't make them go off on their own; sit with them and do the

How Children Succeed

task too so they feel like they have help if they need it.

It can also be beneficial not to force your children to do chores but to encourage them to help around the house. You can ask them if they see anything they can do to clean up the house and let them find a task they are willing to complete. That way you are not engaging in a battle of wills every time you need something completed. If you're having trouble approaching this technique, start by inviting your children to do chores with you, so they don't feel like the burden is entirely on them and they have an opportunity to get one-on-one attention.

CHAPTER 2

Let Them Fail

Do you remember the first time you failed at something? The first F I ever got on a test will forever be burned in my memory. I will never forget that sludge-like feeling that filled my heart when I realized that I had really messed up. I also remember how my parents reacted. I was convinced they would be so angry I'd get yelled at and sent to my room and punished for the next week, but my nine-year-old brain couldn't have been more wrong. They simply asked, "What happened?" I told them I messed up and didn't study for the test. They asked, "Is this going to happen again?" I vehemently shook my head. I never got another F on a test.

If you can try to think back to a time that you failed as a child, you can bet that this is how your child will feel when they fail at something. More importantly, though, think about how you wished your parents would react when you felt that way. Failure is part of life; we cannot protect our children from it no matter how hard we try. In fact, the more we protect them, the less they are able to cope with it. See my parents knew I hadn't studied for that test, but they also knew that telling me to study wouldn't be enough. They had to let me see the consequences of my actions for the lesson to stick.

Failing Is Not Failure

As parents, it can be tempting to want to rescue our children from any negative experience. This can get extreme, such as calling up teachers and asking them to change your child's grades of tests and assignments. Although it feels like protecting your child from emotional harm, it can have reverse effects.

When your child learned how to walk, you saw them fall down a lot. They would fall on their butts, backs, faces, and hands while they wobbled along the street or your kitchen floor. You knew, however, that this was part of the process. You didn't rush over and pick them up every time they fell down because they never would have learned how to walk, and you might end up carrying your 18-year-old at his or her high school graduation. Your child had to fail before they could succeed.

This applies beyond developing basic motor skills, but as the stakes rise, it can become harder for us to let our children fall. Failing a class in school differs greatly from falling over at the park and it's difficult to see what they will learn from that experience. This is when most parents try to step in to save their child's emotions, instead of teaching them how to deal with negative outcomes.

How Children Succeed

Failing at activities can teach children a variety of useful life lessons. First, it gives them an opportunity to learn from their mistakes. When I made an F on that test, I learned that I did not like the way it felt to perform poorly in school, and I made the changes so it would never happen again. If your child doesn't know what failing feels like, they won't know how to work hard to avoid and overcome it.

It also gives children the opportunity to ask others for help, an integral skill in the adult world. No one wants to watch their adult child drown in work because they don't know how to ask other members of their team for help. If we can teach this skill early on, we can avoid this possibility and foster resiliency and a knack for teamwork.

When children are allowed to fail, they can learn that failing at a task doesn't make them a failure as a person. This can be hard to distinguish in the moment, especially for a little kid, but if we can teach them to value their effort despite the results, then we can teach them how to be resilient. They will be able to come back even stronger after setbacks and not be deterred by making mistakes or completely blowing a project.

As parents, we need to resist our urges to make every moment of their lives pleasant. Kids who are regularly protected from failure are typically less motivated to learn and have trouble handling criticism. They might internalize a need for perfection, which can make them more likely to struggle with anxiety or be afraid of changes in their lives and unwilling to try new things.

The world is full of situations in which your child might fail. In fact, everything they do in a day holds the opportunity to fail. Sometimes missing the mark might be their fault, such as when they don't study and fail a test, but sometimes it's out of their control, such as when their team loses a game because they didn't have enough players. You might be a pro at letting them fail in these small areas, but when the stakes get high, it can be harder to hold your tongue.

What if your child has failed every test he's taken so far in school? Your mom-brain is probably already lighting up with ways to get him back on track and monitor his progress and meet with the teacher. Take a breath. This might seem like a crisis, but it can also be an opportunity for growth. The key would be *why* your child is failing; if he or she is not understanding the material, that's one thing, but if he or she is not doing the work, that's another.

In the latter situation, you can view their failure as an opportunity for them to either understand the severity of their situation on their own or learn a difficult lesson. If your child is unwilling to do the work needed to pass fourth grade, then how will he or she find that motivation in fifth grade if you help push him or her along? Sometimes allowing them to face the consequences of their actions is the best way for them to find their own way back onto the right path.

We are not all this strong, however, and a lot of us will cave to swooping in our superhero capes to save the day. You might call the teacher and try to alter his grade or secure a retest, but what is this teaching your child. It shows them they do not need to be responsible for their actions because if negative consequences arise, someone will step in and set things right. This is called "martyr parenting" and it reinforces to your child that they will never have to fight or stand up for themselves.

Using your adult powers to change grades or negotiate with teachers can also show your child that influence is more important than being responsible. They learn that if you can manipulate someone into creating the results you hoped for, then you never have to bear the consequences of negative actions. These ideas can make it difficult for them if carried into adulthood because it might be difficult for them to go far in a job if they can't own up to their own mistakes and are constantly trying to make their boss give them a second chance.

Instead, you can explain the natural consequences to your child to ensure they understand why it happened. Let them know that when they don't study for tests, they are going to fail, and if they continue failing, they will have to repeat the fourth grade. You can offer to help them understand their homework (not by doing it for them), so they know they have your love and support, but ultimately the results are on their shoulders.

"But my child's shoulders are so small," you might think. Trust me, I know. The first time I used this tool, I think I was more upset than my son was about his missed goal in soccer. You will undoubtedly have urges to rescue your child from their own failure; it's part of being a parent. You don't want to see your child struggle, but that is unfortunately part of watching them grow.

In this process, learn which failures are worth the heartbreak and which aren't. If you can learn to distinguish between failure and a crisis, then you will be better equipped to help your child succeed. The first tactic you can use is to establish your parenting end game: do you want your kids to be successful adults or do you want to have to help them forever? I think all of us can say the former is our goal. So when you feel like a terrible mother for letting your child turn in the world's worst science project, remember that you are teaching him or her a valuable lesson that contributes to this end game.

Keep in mind that your child is exactly that: a child. The first time they try something, it will never be perfect; that's the nature of the beast. So even if your child makes a complete mess of a chore the first time they do it—such as flooding the kitchen and then exclaiming they cleaned the dishes—let them own that experience. Encourage them to keep washing the dishes and practice getting the kitchen less wet next time.

Don't forget that children will prioritize the tasks they are praised for, so instead of basing your "great jobs" on the outcome, focus them on how hard your child worked. This can teach them that the work that goes into a task is just as important as if they win or lose. It can help them to not base their own self-worth on whether they got first place.

Sports can be a big part of a child's life and as a parent it might be hard to admit that your kid is not so great at soccer or basketball or whatever you have them enrolled in. Even the outfield grass-pickers and second-base space cadets have parents, though, and they should be proud! The kids are still getting all the benefits of sports such as social interaction and physical activity, so take some time off and let the t-ball game be the arena where you get to just be a fan of your child.

When children struggle in school, it's instinctive to take their side and decide that the teacher is the enemy. This might be the worst mistake you can make, though. Always keep in mind that teachers are just as dedicated to your child's success as you are and there might just be a breakdown of communication. Make time to talk to them and understand the problem fully before deciding on how to proceed with your child. Sometimes a bad grade is what it is, and they have to learn from it.

The Emotional Response

Failing isn't fun and there is no way to make your kid think so. All you can do is take the time to help them understand why they failed and try to reframe the experience as something positive. If you make it a point to love and support your child even when he or she fails, then it will make them more confident when they have to attempt a similar task because they know you will be there for them no matter what.

There are a few definitive things you can do to promote this positive mindset. Clarifying that risk-taking is a family value is one of them. When your child goes out on a limb to accomplish something, such as joining an art contest in an advanced age group, celebrate his or her decision to do something challenging even if they lose.

You can also teach your children that there is a natural adjustment period when everyone starts something new. If they have been assigned a new chore, you can say, "I don't expect you to do it perfectly, but please try your best." This prepares them for the inevitable micro failures of performing a new task and not taking honest mistakes as huge faults. It also teaches them they shouldn't give up if they aren't perfect at something on the first try.

Sometimes, your child will take failure very seriously. It will seem like his or her entire world is falling apart, and you will have the primal desire to make it all okay. In these instances, try to come up with constructive ways you can help your child understand why they didn't succeed. You can go back through the chain of events and encourage them to find where things went wrong, so next time they can adjust their behavior in the moment.

Giving them some independence can, ironically, be an effective way to support them. This works especially well with school. Let them be responsible for keeping up with homework, projects, and deadlines, as these are all skills they will need in the adult world. Make sure you are still asking questions about their day and what subject they enjoyed most, but let them take the lead on meeting their educational requirements.

Considering the words we use to describe failure can also help to create a more positive mindset around not coming out on top. For example, instead of telling your child, "You lost the game, but it's okay," you can try saying, "You put in a really great effort tonight and tried your best." This takes the focus off of the negative aspect of the situation and highlights the positive things your child did. It teaches them not to focus on the failure but celebrate the success of having made it there.

Unfortunately, sometimes your child will not do a good job, plain and simple. Not every parent, especially mothers, has the heart to look their child in the eye and tell them they did not perform well. Sometimes that's exactly what they need, though. You don't have to be mean or condescending, but if you could tell they did not put out their best effort, you can ask if they think they tried their hardest and let them come to the conclusion themselves.

No matter how hard you try to stay strong and let your child be their own person, it's difficult to watch them fail. It might even affect you more than it affects your child, like it did with me. It's just not in our nature to watch our child fall flat on their face and stay calmly on the sidelines while they pick themselves up. We want to help; we want to protect; we want to make it all better. It can be important for parents to address their own emotions about their child failing to be prepared when the time comes.

The first thing to prepare yourself for is the anxiety that comes with letting your child fail. Today's society seems to link the success of your children to your parental efficacy, so negative effects for your son or daughter can feel like they are happening to you. You might feel embarrassed or upset as if you were the one who failed, but remember that you can regulate those emotions and your child—depending on how old they are—

cannot. Let your emotions be an opportunity to show your child how to act in the face of negative feelings.

It can also be helpful to take moments to practice self-compassion. Being a mother is *hard*. You never feel like you've done enough, there's always one child screaming, and somehow the dirty laundry pile grows every time you wash a load. We all get caught up in the negative thought cycles of "I'm not good enough" or "I'm failing as a mom," but these are not true. You are enough. Believe that. Make a list of all the things you do for your family during the week and you'll see how valued you are. Start a mantra look at this list and say "I am a good parent" until you sincerely believe it.

Letting your child fail is one thing, but getting wrapped up in their negative consequences is something you can control. It might take a little time to adjust to the mindset that failing is okay, and it doesn't make you a failure. You teach your kids the same thing: when you start something new you won't be perfect. So try to take your own advice, find a way to calm down, gain your focus, and support your child through the good and the bad in life.

CHAPTER 3

Make Your Kids Read Daily and Learn Math at an Early Age

All of my children are reluctant to practice math, but eager to eat cookies. So, as all good parents, I trick them. They are allowed to eat three cookies when I make them, and I have them count out how many they've eaten. If my five-year-old has had two cookies, I'll ask him how many more he is allowed to have. While he's figuring out how many cookies to eat, he's also working math skills in his brain. It's a win-win.

Obviously, we can't bribe our children every time we need them to practice a skill, so I've also outlined some great ways to make them do it on their own. Reading and math help children develop critical skills such as problem solving, empathy, and literacy. Therefore, it can be so important to establish routines that help them practice these skills every day. Things such as making dedicated quiet time for reading, or toys that help them practice counting and recognizing numbers can make these skills commonplace and less intimidating when they need to use them.

Benefits of Learning Basic Skills

Reading and math might seem like opposite ends of the educational spectrum, but they utilize a lot of the same skills. Children have to learn how to associate meaning to both letters and numbers as they grow, which can work the problem-solving center of their brain. If you can emphasize these skills when your child is young, then they can start ahead of the curve in school and be sure to keep up with their classmates.

Children who read regularly will naturally advance their skills as they age. The more they are exposed to it, the more they can practice and learn. Reading works the brain significantly more than watching television or playing video games because it is a more complex task. Instead of being fed information on a screen, children have to distinguish sounds and patterns to understand a book.

Because reading requires this extra layer of attention, it can help to improve a child's concentration. When you first read to your squirmy two-year-old, it might seem like they can never sit through one page of a picture book, much less the whole thing. As you continue the ritual of sitting down with them and reading the book whether or not they are sitting, they will tune in. Eventually, they will want to see what you are looking at and take an interest in the book.

Watching you read will develop their vocabulary, language skills, and attention span.

Reading can also help to develop a child's imagination and empathy. We love to watch our children play pretend in the backyard or in their room and reading gives them fuel for their creative fires. Stories can spark ideas in their minds and show them all the possibilities in the world. They can also show your child how to care for people. Children's books often mention emotions or show it in the illustrations because children are so attuned to nonverbal cues. When they see a sad character, they can identify that they would be sad in the situation too.

Learning basic math principles at an early age can give your child the foundation to accomplish things in all aspects of their life. In fact, these skills can be the make-it-or break-it factor of future academic success.

Even introducing the concept of numbers and counting when your child is an infant and throughout their early years can help them have a better grasp on math when they start school. This is because you teach them how to think of the world with a problem-solving mindset, so they go into challenges with a confident and open mind. With this foundation, they will have an easier time grasping ideas such as addition and subtraction when they are introduced to it in school because they already understand the value of numbers. Having that fully formed thought process can make math much simpler than for children who do not really understand what numbers represent.

You might think this is an impossible task to ask of a young child. Don't expect your toddler to be completing advanced calculus at his or her coloring table, but believe that they can understand the basic concepts of elementary mathematics. Scientists have found that even six-month-olds have a sense of the value of numbers and amounts, so your three-year-old can definitely understand if they are given the opportunity.

Perhaps the most interesting thing about math and reading for children, is that they both rely primarily on memory retrieval. This is no simple skill for a child either, it requires teamwork between their reasoning ability, memory, attention span, and a host of other mental functions. For example, an attentive child might not be good at reading, but he or she will probably be able to recall all the words in their story. As a parent, we might think of this as cheating, but it's helping your child's reading skills because they are still associating words with the pictures in the book if not the letters and words themselves. In time, they will make it down to mechanics, but for now let them rattle off the story of a little boy who bought a pig as many times as they'd like.

It can still be tricky to know the right time to introduce these skills. You might worry that your child isn't able to understand the concepts (which they probably are) or that they might not like you if you force them to practice (which they definitely won't). Just like reading to your baby in infancy can have its benefits, showing them numbers and amounts does too.

As they get older, you'll surely be looking to make sure they are keeping up with their friends in school. If your child is a little behind, however, don't panic. All children learn at different rates, and your child might just seem behind because they are having trouble focusing in school. Keep an eye out to ensure they are hitting all of their developmental milestones and they will come around to the curve in their own time.

Some important reading milestones that you can look for is recognizing rhymes and understanding that letters stand for sounds, even if they don't know the correct sound. Children should be able to do this sometimes around kindergarten and build on the skills so they can begin reading in first grade.

How Children Succeed

If your child can master how to read, it can even help them in math. Do you remember those confusing word problems your teachers used to stick in your math tests? They still exist! But if a child is great at math and not at reading, then they might still get the problem wrong because they don't understand what is being asked of them. This is why these skills are important to build at the same time.

Your child will inevitably have strengths and weaknesses in school. The important thing is that you listen to which subjects they don't like or might struggle with and help them find the underlying problem. If you can identify that, you can find the skills you need to continue to work on helping them get better.

How to Help

One of the biggest obstacles you might face with your child when you try to encourage reading is a lack of motivation. If your child is squirming when you sit down with a book, or flat out refusing to listen to you read or to read themselves, then they might struggle with something more than just not wanting to sit still. They might find reading challenging and are having trouble expressing their frustration in other ways, so try to stay patient and ask them why they don't want to read. They might tell you it's too difficult or that they think it's boring. Figure out which parts they find difficult or boring and help them develop the skills to get through them with confidence. You can help them sound out words they are having trouble identifying or take them to the library to pick out books that interest them.

To start a routine at home, setting aside dedicated reading time can be a great start. If left to their own devices, children will probably ask to watch television or play games when they are bored, not read. So if you have a special time during the day when they know they have to either read or sit quietly, it can encourage them to pick up a book just as a way of entertainment. Once they are in the habit of reading, they will get better at it and want to read on their own. It's also a great way for you to make sure they are being exposed to reading skills every day.

During dedicated reading time, your child can read aloud so they put together their sounds with their letters. It can also help to generate their interest in reading because it is an opportunity to impress you with their abilities. They will grab a book happily and show you how much progress they have made in identifying words, rhymes, and patterns.

If your child is a squirmy wormy who has trouble sitting still, then you can create a special area in your house just for reading. Decorate it with colors and comfortable seating like bean bags or a tiny child-sized recliner so they feel like it is a fun cozy place to hang out. You can put all of their books in this area either on a bookshelf or in creative stacks and buckets. Encourage them to spend time in their nook, reading and exploring different worlds that they can tell you all about when they finish their book.

A key to the reading area being a success is to provide books that are on par with your child's reading abilities, so they never feel discouraged by books that are too difficult for them. You can also add in tons of books related to what your child is interested in so he or she will be motivated to read and learn. If he or she loves cars, you can get picture books about cars and trucks or books about how cars work. Periodically, take them with you to buy new books and let them see if there is anything else they are interested in reading about.

If you have multiple children, you can even let the older siblings read to your younger ones. This has double benefits because it makes the older siblings feel more responsible and important while also developing language skills for all the kids. Plus kids are more likely to hang out with their siblings than with us.

Slipping math into your child's daily routine can be a little trickier. Before starting school, most children have a basic understanding of mathematical principles such as addition and

How Children Succeed

subtraction from joining you in the world. They might be aware these things exist, but getting them to understand the value behind it is a separate endeavor.

When your child eventually starts school, there are a few key concepts their classes will focus on such as counting, representation, measurement, spatial awareness, estimation, and patterns. Counting helps kids to develop a sense of numbers and what they mean, plus it's an easy tool to develop when they are still primarily in your care. When you buy things in the grocery store like bananas, you can count how many bananas are in your bunch so your child can understand that a number correlates with an amount.

Representation is another easy skill to teach them, even when they are infants. Using shape sorter toys and puzzles with animals or other shapes can give them a sense of how shapes relate to each other. (It also has the added bonus of developing matching skills.) As they look at the toy in their hand, they have to identify the shape to make the game work and get the block where it goes. This helps in identifying shapes in school and recognizing how they relate to each other, such as two triangles making a square.

As your toddler gets a little older, around three or four years old, you can even teach them your phone number or your address. This also helps them realize that numbers in a certain pattern has meaning. They can memorize all the numbers in your phone number, but if they are in the wrong order, you won't get their call. Just like if they have the numbers right for their house but told the bus driver backwards, they might end up on the opposite side of your neighborhood.

Make math a part of your child's daily life by pointing out the size of things to help them understand measurements. If you're walking down a path and your child finds two sticks, ask them which is bigger or to find one that is smaller than the smallest stick. This can help them think

How Children Succeed

critically about size and measurement and will make beginning math a breeze.

Allowing your kids to pitch in in the kitchen can be the best way to teach them about math—and they won't even know they're learning! Cooking is all about measuring, doubling, halfing, and mixing. You can show them how you measure amounts of ingredients and ask them how you could make more from a recipe. Letting them stir can show them that when you combine amounts, you get more than you started with, and if you take some out, you'll have less.

Take walks with your children, too, because the world is full of math, there for the figuring. You can ask your child to guess how far away the park is, and you might be surprised by their answers. You could ask them to compare two cars in a driveway or similarities between two different plants. Remember, math isn't all about formulas and equations, it's also these basic little tasks that we perform every day and can easily turn into a fun game.

CHAPTER 4

Set High Expectations

I am always amazed by the things my kids accomplish without any help from me. These little people that I see as being so fragile and small are fierce, smart, and competitive people with an iron will. They can do so much more than I remember doing at their age and my heart swells with pride every time they succeed. This is no coincidence, though. In our home, my husband and I have made a point to set high expectations for our children and let them rise to the occasion.

When you look down at your child and see the baby you were holding such a short time ago, it can be difficult to remember that they are a whole person. Part of you might always see them as that helpless infant, but most of you need to realize that they are itching for a challenge. Setting the bar high can encourage children to tackle challenges with excitement and stick with difficult tasks until they succeed. If they know what is expected of them, their desire to please will carry them through to success.

Benefits of High Expectations

Children tend to rise to the expectations of their parents, no matter how high the stakes. If their parents expect them to go to college, they go to college. If their parents expect them to do well in school, they do. It seems to be all about communicating what you want and then letting your child do the work with repercussions for poor behavior. In fact, this approach seems to be directly related to children's success. Kids who grow up in "hands off" parenting environments are more likely to turn to drug use and have a negative relationship with their parents. Kids raised in a "hands on" parenting environment, those that established expectations and enforced consequences for negative behavior, typically succeeded as adults and had good relationships with their parents.

Parental expectations have the most influence on a child's performance in school, even more than teachers'. Children whose parents expected high achievements were less likely to drop out of school than children whose parents did not set clear or high expectations for their academic performance.

Setting academic expectations is not the only way to boost your child's performance in life, though. They also need clear behavioral expectations to understand how you expect them to relate to and treat others. This can help them be more respectful students, friends, and have more patience to pay attention when others are speaking. When a child understands what is expected of them, it can make them feel more confident when they approach challenging situations because they have guidelines to follow instead of having to look to negative influences for behavioral cues.

They can also take more responsibility for their actions because they knew they were doing something wrong when they acted out. They cannot hide behind the excuse that you never told them not to when your expectations were outlined years ago. Possessing this level of maturity can help them become leaders in their class and on teams because they understand owning mistakes and learning from them.

Part of setting these high expectations is to help your children develop the skills they will need to meet them. For example, if your son has ADHD and you expect him to sit still and quietly during school, take time in the afternoon or morning to help him get some of his energy out and practice paying attention and being respectful. This helps him know that you are not setting him up for failure and will help him reach his goals.

Maybe your main concern is encouraging your child to make all A's in school. After all, that is every parent's dream, isn't it? We all want to put our children in the best schools so they can have the best education, but have you ever stopped to think what makes one school better than another? What do we look for when we determine a school's worth? The answer is high expectations.

Schools that require exemplary academic and behavioral standards are typically the ones rated higher. This is because they set the bar for students to live up to and if they don't there are serious repercussions, such as being suspended or expelled. These clear expectations drives their students to achieve higher test scores and gain entry to prestigious colleges. They know what they have to do to succeed in the environment, so they put in the work to get there.

How Children Succeed

Unfortunately, this standard is not applied in all schools. Our children will inevitably end up in a less-than-ideal situation at one time or another so they will need our help to stay focused on the endgame. Don't be worried if your child isn't in a top-rated school or hasn't won any state titles for being the smartest kid. Although teachers and the school's attitude can make a difference in a child's behavior and performance, time and time again, they will look back to their parents.

Your expectations are more important to your child than their teacher's expectations. This shows that even if your child isn't in the prestigious prep club in the swanky part of town, you can still help them achieve just as much as the students who go there. The key is to have the same expectations at home as they would get from an expensive, top-notch school, and you will get the same results.

Setting these expectations can get tricky, though, because you don't want to confuse them with standards. When your expectations are high, your child knows the core sets of values you believe and how you expect them to adhere to those values. When your standards are high, you are expecting a certain quality of work from your child. Although there is nothing inherently wrong with setting standards for work, you want to make sure they are reasonable and match your child's abilities. For example, if your child is not great at art then it can be difficult for them if your standard of acceptable work is a piece that could claim first prize. Instead, you can expect them to do their best work and they will know that even if it's not perfect, you are still proud of them.

Having expectations instead of high standards is much easier on your child's emotions. They want to live up to everything you ask of them, so we have to make sure we are setting the bar high with concrete examples of how to please us. High standards can cause undue stress and make it more difficult for them to focus on learning and developing new talents because they are too concerned with making everything perfect.

How Children Succeed

I know this can be a delicate differentiation to make as a parent, so it might take some time for you to assess accurately where your child's skill level is. You can take some time at the beginning of the school to let your kids' show you all the things they did in school, and you will get a good idea of where their strengths are. That way, as the year goes on, you will be able to tell which assignments they phoned in and which they did their very best on. If you're in touch with your child and know which subjects their hearts are in, you will have no trouble giving them attainable expectations.

How to Hold Expectations

There are a few tricks to setting expectations that your child can rise to, without having a lot of unnecessary bumps in the road first. It might feel like you're making obscure requests when you start, but if you can implement some key elements of expectation-setting, then you and your child will be on the same page.

First, you want to make sure they are attainable, but not so easy that they don't require effort. You have to find that sweet spot. This isn't expected for the first go-round, though, so don't start panicking yet. It might take a few weeks or even months for you to find a reasonable level of expectation for your child, so allow for that trial and error. If your child hasn't been able to meet your expectations after a few months, then you might need to adjust them to his or her level. Or if they soar over them in a few days, then you probably want to raise the stakes a bit.

Unreasonable expectations can be harmful to your kids, which is why it's so important to take as much time as you need on the first step. They might start to feel like they can never make you proud of them if they can't meet your beliefs of their talent. This could lead to them thinking they aren't good enough and having a diminished self-esteem. To avoid this, talk to your child and try to understand how he or she feels about the situation. Oftentimes, it's difficult for a child to tell their parent that they can't please them, so if your child seems dejected offer a solution yourself. It can be as simple as saying, "Do you feel like I'm pushing you too hard?"

On the opposite side of this problem, make sure you aren't underestimating your children either. Just like toddlers can do more chores than we think, your child can do more than just what you see. If we don't encourage our children to take on challenges and work through tough situations, who will? As we all know, our kids pick up on everything. If your child thinks you don't believe they can succeed at something, odds are they won't believe it either. Pick an area where your child needs to improve and set incremental goals for them, that way they know you expect them not to be the best, but to get better.

To get our kids on board with all these new strategies, we need to make sure we are communicating. Just like in your spousal relationship, it takes communication to make expectations effective. When your child starts the school year or a new sport, make sure you are specific about what you hope they get out of it and achieve. For example, don't tell your kids "I want you to do well in school," tell them "I want you to make all A's this year." This gives them something concrete they can work toward.

Children ultimately learn by watching you, so don't forget about your nonverbal communication. Make sure you are modeling the behavior you want from them and meeting your own expectations every day. This shows them that there aren't arbitrary rules imposed on them and the entire family is expected to push themselves to the best they can be.

Helping your child achieve their goals can be one of the most difficult parts of this exercise. You want to let them do things on their own, but sometimes they need a little push or some extra help to reach the winner's podium. The main encouragement you can offer is believing in their abilities.

How Children Succeed

Think about a time when you had a lofty goal or task to attain at work; it was probably pretty intimidating to think about before you started. Did your boss encourage you through the project? Did your coworkers help to make sure everything was right? This is how your child feels and it's what they need when you set high expectations: they need the same support you did to succeed.

Your child will continually find ways to achieve their goals, so make plans for next steps before they get there. Don't let one accomplishment be the end of the road. Find logical steppingstones for them to follow to make it to a new skill or mastery of an old one. With every step, all the guidelines of setting expectations apply: make sure it's appropriate, communicate it clearly, and support your child. As they achieve these small goals, be sure to celebrate their success so they will stay motivated to keep moving forward.

CHAPTER 5

Praise Them Correctly

Is there any better sight in the world than watching your child's face light up when you tell them "good job" or "congratulations?" I think not. The way their little faces light up with joy and their eyes get wide as if to ask if you really mean it never fails to warm my heart. It almost makes praising as fun for the parents as it is for the kids. Even with this influx of adorableness, we need to make sure we aren't praising them too often.

Kids take praise as a reinforcement for certain

behaviors, but they also know when they deserve it and when they don't. For example, if I praised my seven-year-old for using the toilet in the bathroom, he'd probably look at me like I was crazy. That's because we all know he's capable of and expected to use the bathroom like a grown-up. The same goes for all age groups. They know which things they are capable of and if you praise them for everyday accomplishments, then they won't value it when it's deserved. That's why this chapter outlines the right way and time to praise your child and how to develop an appropriate mindset.

The Right Mindset

Everything your child does might seem amazing, especially when they're young and learning things for the first time. But if you praise their every action all their lives, it can backfire. The more praise they receive the more they expect until eventually they need to be praised for everything they do, and the reaction loses its importance.

So you might think, "Okay, don't overpraise. Simple." Not so simple. There are also wrong ways to praise a child. (I know. I thought it sounded crazy when I first learned too.). Some parents might inadvertently focus their praise on themselves, such as saying "I think you did awesome." This statement tells your child you approve of their performance and can lead to approval-seeking behaviors. Instead, you can focus on making your child the focus of your praise with statements such as, "I bet you're proud of how well you did!" This way they know that their performance is something to admire, and you noticed their effort.

Your mindset makes a big difference when you offer praise to your children. There are two ways to look at situations: with a fixed mindset or a growth mindset. A fixed mindset means you believe that your natural skills are what they are and can't be changed. For example, if your child is good at soccer and bad at baseball, you would believe that he or she was meant to play soccer. A growth mindset, however, acknowledges that hard work can pay off and develop weaker skills. You would encourage your child to keep practicing baseball until they got better at it.

Setting this tone for your children can be as easy as the words you use to praise them. If you praise the end result or only things they excel in, then your child might think they will never be good at other things they struggle with. If you praise them for working on a skill they want to develop, then they will know that they have the potential to get better. This can help them feel more confident when they tackle new challenges and be willing to learn new skills.

A growth mindset can also make your child more optimistic and open to criticism. This is because they understand the value of hard work and that they can't do everything on their own. It can also make your job a lot easier as a parent if your child is excited to do new things instead of dreading it.

Another way to foster this way of thinking is to make sure you praise the way your children approach a problem. It might not even have been a successful process, however, because they thought outside of the box for a solution that is an accomplishment. If you can reinforce this way of thinking, then your children can apply their creativity to any problem in their life. For example, if your child found a unique mnemonic device to remember how to solve a math problem, let them know what a smart idea it is. Then when they advance in school and are hit with harder subjects and projects, they will know tricks to help their brain hold all the information.

When you praise at appropriate times, it can even help you shape your child's behavior. Your children learn how to behave based on the way you react to their actions, so if you take time to praise good behavior then they will see the pattern to their rewards. Focusing on the positive behavior instead of the negative behavior can help you establish your expectations because your child will repeat the actions that drew your behavior. So instead of yelling and fussing when your child is misbehaving at a party, thank another child for sitting quietly and waiting their turn.

Certain behaviors are especially keen to praise, such a social skills, compliance, and effort. Taking the time to praise your child when they are sharing with others or waiting their turn on the playground can help them realize that these are appropriate ways to be friends with others. When you thank them for sitting still and listening to your instructions, then they will want to continue doing that when you talk because they know it makes you happy. If they are working hard to develop a new skill and you support them along the way, they are more likely to put in the effort to make it to the end.

Our children have short attention spans, as we all learned the first time we wanted them to sit and read a book with us. Because of this, if you are planning to use praise to promote certain behaviors, be sure you dole out the compliments immediately after the behavior and frequently to reinforce the idea. If you wait too long, your child will forget what action you are talking about and have a harder time discerning what he or she did right. Also, if you praise them for throwing away their plate once, the next time he or she does it, they'll be looking for the same reaction to make sure it's still a good thing.

Eventually, you will run out of ways to say "good job." To keep your kid on his or her toes, you can also thank him for exhibiting good behaviors. This helps to know that good behavior is appreciated by others and can make other people feel good too. For example, if your child just washed all the dishes in the sink, instead of telling them they did a great job, you can thank them for contributing to the household chores.

Praise in Action

This might seem like a lot to take in, so let's look at practical ways you can praise your child in the

How Children Succeed

moment. The most important thing to remember is that not every action requires praise. Let your kid learn that a certain amount of effort is required to impress you so they will start working to accomplish difficult things. If you praise every little thing that your child does, then they might feel like they have to impress you to get affection, which is not true.

When you praise your children, make sure you are specific with what makes you happy. For example, your daughter might draw a beautiful picture of your family playing soccer on a sunny day. Instead of complimenting the picture, you can point out how she took her time drawing the grass and did a great job showing how the family members were running. This lets them know you are taking the time to examine their work, and it encourages them to keep at this activity.

It can be difficult for younger children to distinguish what they did to earn praise, so if you are specific it can increase your chances of reinforcing good behavior. If your toddler behaved well at his or her friend's birthday party and you thank them for being so good, they won't be able to pinpoint the behaviors that made you happy, so the effects will not be as significant. If you tell him or her that you are proud of how they asked to share toys and helped their friend when they fell down, then your child can link those specific actions with the praise they are receiving.

Focus on the positive moments with your kids instead of fixating on the bad ones. So much of parenting can be correcting, fussing, yelling, or putting your child on a timeout. It makes you feel like you are always the disciplinarian and never the mom. That's why it can be important for you and your child to take time to acknowledge the positive things during the day. If they're being quiet in the car, thank them for giving you a peaceful drive, or if they say please and thank you appreciate their politeness. This helps to set a positive tone and let them know that negative consequences do not have to be the routine if they behave.

How Children Succeed

I am the first to admit that I love bragging about my children. I think we all do sometimes. We work so hard to make these little people, so when they do well, we want a little praise for our efforts, too (after all we're all just big kids at heart, right?). Doing this in front of them can put a lot of pressure on their little minds, though. They might hear you call them a soccer star and feel like they have to be great in every game to live up to that title. It's okay to let people know how well your child is doing or if they're improving in an area, but if they're around be sure they're listening to which qualities you brag about.

Families with divorced and married parents alike can still face similar communication problems. Sometimes the mom might not see the dad until 6 p.m. when he gets home from work, or only on Saturdays when he comes to pick up the kids for the weekend. Either way, making sure both parents know about the child's achievements can really boost your child's reaction. It's one thing to have mom's approval, but when mom and dad both get on board, it's like winning an Olympic gold medal. So keep your spouse or partner in the loop so they can congratulate your children, too.

Be honest with your children when you give them feedback. If they do a poor job and then look to you for praise, don't congratulate them just to save their self-esteem. They need to hear an honest opinion so they can both improve their work and learn how to take constructive criticism. Remember that your body language says a lot about what you think, too. Children can see from how you position yourself and react if you are telling the truth. So when you are excited, make sure to show it in your face and posture by smiling and standing up tall and proud.

Praise can often come in the form of encouragement because at the heart, that's usually what it is. The most common phrases we use to encourage our kids can send the wrong message, though. Luckily, there are ways we can adjust our words and our message to have a more positive effect.

How Children Succeed

"Good job" is probably the most used phrase among parents. We use it as affirmation for everything from doing chores, to helping friends, to making it to the top of the playground. But what does it really mean? For kids, it's hard to tell. So try to be as specific as you can when you feel the urge to say, "good job." try saying "Good job helping your friend."

Other popular words of encouragement are "You did it!" Without meaning to, you are praising the outcome of your child's actions instead of the effort. Try to replace this phrase with acknowledgments of how they worked to achieve whatever they accomplished. "You've been practicing for two weeks and you just rode your bike on your own. I bet you're proud!"

How cute are your kids? Pretty darn cute, right? I bet every now and then you exclaim just how cute they look in their tiny school uniform or with their new shoes on because, honestly, it's hard to contain yourself in those moments. Try to make sure, though, that you don't consistently praise your child for the way they look. This can lead to low self-esteem because after a while they might think they are only valued for the way they look. Instead of telling them how cute they are, ask them what their favorite part of their school outfit is, or why they picked out those new shoes.

Remember the fixed mindset from earlier? When we praise children for fixed skills such as intelligence, you can inadvertently promote a fixed mindset. Statements like "You're so smart," or "You'll go to Harvard one day" relay the information that their intelligence is the star not their work. You can still congratulate a good grade, but just make sure to slip in a comment about how hard they worked to earn it.

Some kids are picky eaters or refuse to eat at mealtimes, so it can be tempting to get excited when they eat all the food on their plate. Although you mean to encourage eating when you want them to, praising children for eating can lead to them developing a negative relationship with it. They might think they need to eat to please others or that they are not supposed to respect their body's hunger signals. If your child struggles to eat all of their food at once, then take their plate when they are finished and let them know if they get hungry later you can warm it up for them (except bedtimes if it becomes a distraction).

CHAPTER 6

Help Them Build Meaningful Relationships

Kids seem to be the best at making friends. It's almost as if it comes naturally to them. They carry less of the baggage that adult carry, but their social skills can still vary on the lessons they've learned. Children learn from our example and how they interact with us early in their lives. When we encourage them to say "Hi" to people and play with other children, they develop that confidence that so many of us admire. They find their gumption to walk up to a new kid, introduce themselves, and immediately launch into a fantasy game.

There are certain things that we, as parents, can do to help our kids develop these necessary social skills. We need to make sure we encourage social situations and give our children the opportunity to play with us. If we teach our children how to be polite, manage their feelings, and trust others then there is no situation they won't be confident enough to tackle.

Creating Healthy Relationships

Humans are social beings, which means that we need relationships to help us feel like we are part of a group. This innate desire starts in our children and can be a powerful thing. The friendships they form early in their lives can help them develop social skills and feel loved and accepted. These feelings will carry into adulthood and be the building blocks for more healthy relationships.

The first two years of a child's life is typically the most formative regarding their mental health. Positive relationships are imperative during these years because it can teach them how they should expect to be treated by others and what their worth is. The parent-child and caregiver relationships are the most important because these are the people they will see most often and associate with their own well-being. During this time, they need a consistent, loving relationship that is sensitive to their needs and wants so they can learn how to form a trusting bond with someone.

As your children grow, they will use the skills they saw you implement in your relationships. Just like you hugged your daughter when she cried, she will hug her friends when they cry. Just like you read her a book when she was upset, she will try to read a book to her friend who is mad. This is why making sure you always model a loving, healthy relationship can be especially important for your children.

The parent-child relationship also affects the way your child views relationships, such as whether they are good or bad things. It nurtures every aspect of their being—social, physical, and emotional—so the messages received are deep-seated. If they have always had a positive relationship with you, then they will expect all of their relationships to be just as nurturing and likely work to make them so.

This relationship will also be the foundation of your child's personality and behavior. You can even notice this between siblings sometimes. You have tons of time to spend with your first child, nurturing and teaching them the ways of the world. With your second child, however, you might not have the same undivided attention to give them every day. As they get older, your oldest child might be more invested in making you part of their playtime and showing you what they did during the day, while your youngest might tend to be more independent.

Children who grow up surrounded by happy and secure relationships are more likely to learn how to regulate their emotions under stress and to be optimistic and confident in social situations. They grew up watching your emotions and how you handled them so when the time comes for them to experience anger or joy for the first time, they know how to work through that feeling. Because they grew up knowing they were loved and valued, they go into new friendships assuming the other person will do the same, so they are not intimidated.

Building your relationship with your children as they age is important, so you want to know that you're doing what's best for them. It's hard to gauge your relationship if you spend most of your time orchestrating the delicate symphony that is your home life, but there are some things you can do to make sure your child feels connected to you.

How Children Succeed

Having unstructured time to spend with your child during the day, especially when they are young, can help them feel closer to you. Take an hour or so after school or before going to soccer practice to sit with your child, without distractions, and let them tell you what they feel like doing. They might ask you to color with them or play pretend or teach them how to do something. The key is to let them take the lead in this time, so they feel like you are tuned in to their needs and listening to them, which builds love and trust.

Show an interest in your child's passions as they grow. Some of the most dreaded words a parent can hear from their child is "You just don't understand me!" Avoid this scenario by making sure you ask questions about the things they're interested in and follow up occasionally to see if their interests have changed. If you take the time to let them describe it to you, then you can better understand why they love it and encourage them to keep pursuing it.

Children have big emotions that can be difficult for them to process, so teaching them healthy ways to express these feelings can be beneficial. The ways they can express their feelings will depend on how old your children are, so keep in mind that you will have to continue teaching them as they age. Once you show them the appropriate ways to handle their feelings, encourage them to use the skills you've taught them. If they yell and throw their toys, ask them to use their words and remember what you taught them so they can practice emotional regulation.

When you encourage your child to express their feelings, you also need to respect their feelings. Remember, their emotions are as real as yours and mine and we need to teach them that people should respect their boundaries. If your child is upset with you and says they want to be left alone, as hard as it may be, leave them alone. Tell them where you will be there when they are ready to talk and that you love them even if they're mad. This way they know that being upset doesn't mean affection is taken away, and also, they are entitled to their space if they feel that they need it.

Another part of being a parent is holding the burden for introducing new relationships into your child's life. This can be by sending to them daycare or school, or bringing them to parties at a new person's house where they don't know all the other children. It might seem simpler to take your child to the park on your own, but making time for playdates can encourage your child to seek out new friends on their own. When they do this, they learn which behaviors, such as introducing themselves and taking turns, help them make friends.

Family, however, is the first and strongest line of support in our lives starting from the moment we are born. Building a strong bond with your children and family members is an easy way to create an accepting atmosphere for your child. This will help them identify healthy relationships as they grow.

We all know families can be difficult. Having so many people who care about you spread out across the town, state, or country can be amazing and taxing. It's hard to keep up with everyone and even harder to make sure you speak to everyone regularly. If you live far from your family, or don't have time to spend with them often, don't feel bad. Your child won't suffer any ill effects if they don't see their grandparents every day. You can, however, attempt to talk to your relatives with your child at least once or twice a month. This can help your child see that there is a whole network of people cheering them on and can help them to develop their communication skills by talking with people of all ages.

This also provides an opportunity for you to teach your child how to listen. We've all had a day when we started talking and our child never even bothered to look up at us. When you video chat or are on a phone call, model good listening skills. Have your child practice sitting still, looking at the person in the eye, and answering questions they are asked. It can also teach them the value of putting away distractions when someone wants to have a conversation with them.

Communication also shows children how to practice empathy and express their own feelings. To further encourage this, you can make it a policy to use "I" messages in your home when communicating feelings. This keeps family members from placing blame on others and gives them a way to express their emotions. It can help children learn that it is okay to take responsibility for their feelings.

If your child struggles with expressing their emotions, you can create a safe space in your home where the whole family shares their feelings. Making this a group activity can help your child feel less scared or intimidated. When your child can express themselves appropriately at home, it means they can also do so in the real world.

Fostering Social Skills

Childhood relationships can be important; some people even keep their childhood friends for their entire lives. These friendships can help young children and older children alike develop a range of social skills that will serve them well in adulthood. This is where they learn how to cooperate, compromise, and apologize before the stakes get too high. Friendships can be a significant factor in your child developing a sensitivity to others' viewpoints and learning how to have a successful conversation.

Daycare and preschool friends can help your child to learn emotional skills that help them feel like they're a part of a group. Children are especially attuned to someone who is acting nice or mean, and they don't let people push them around. To make friends with a kid in their class, your child will learn that they have to be nice and respectful to be part of the group. When they start to feel a sense of belonging early in life, it can help them keep it when they grow up and reduce the likelihood of them feeling isolated or depressed when they might not have a group of friends, such as moving to a new town.

Friends can also influence your child's academic performance—in a good way—and help each other correct poor behavior in school. If you know that your child struggles to sit still in his kindergarten class, try encouraging a friendship with someone you've noticed behaves well. This kid can then show your child how to act in class and they can help each other with activities or homework.

Sometimes your child's friends will move away or go to a new school, and that can be a difficult transition. When my kids switched schools after we moved, they were devastated to lose their friends, even though they knew they'd make new ones. As a parent, you can help them stay connected to the people who matter to them. Sit down with them and write a letter to their friend, or let them use your phone to call them. You can even invite their friend to stay the weekend with you, if you're still within driving distance. Showing your child that you can always be connected with those you love will teach them that sometimes it's worth it to put a little extra effort into a relationship.

Eventually your baby girl or boy will reach the age when they want to date. It's every parent's worst nightmare, but there are ways to get through it. If you've modeled healthy relationships and taught them the skills they need to express themselves, then they will be well-equipped to navigate the dating world.

Make sure you are always modeling self-respect and healthy boundaries to show your child what is appropriate in a relationship. It might seem obvious to us not to date someone who makes you feel bad about yourself, but for kids it's difficult to balance strong emotions that only yield negative results. If they've spent their lives watching you stay away from people who don't value you, though, they will understand that this is not a healthy way to care for someone.

How Children Succeed

Teens have a way of losing themselves in their relationships. Remember your first boyfriend or girlfriend and how you thought they hung the moon? To keep your teen or preteen from venturing too far into someone else's personality, encourage their sense of self as early as you can. Be open to their interests and let them know that those are what make them unique. When your child has a strong sense of self, it will be more difficult for them to get lost in others' influences.

Supporting inclusion and diversity can also help your child to feel more secure in themselves. After all, there are no "cool" kids and "weird" kids, just a bunch of different kids. If you can celebrate the word "different" and show them that every person has value, no matter their interests, skin color, or heritage, then your child can worry less about being popular and more about being themselves.

Enjoying So Far?

I hope you are enjoying reading this book so far! I hope you are enjoying reading the book so far, please let me know how much you like it. You are more than welcome to review the book now or after you are done reading! Now let's get back to the book...

CHAPTER 7

Teach Them to Be Healthy

We all want our kids to grow up "healthy, wealthy, and wise." Although the latter two depends on your child, you can often be in control of their physical health. Creating healthy habits such as a balanced diet and regular exercise start when we are young. If we can build a routine for our children, then they will carry that desire to eat well and feel good throughout their lives. Not that you can stop eating at McDonald's forever when you're in a pinch, but just focusing on cooking healthy meals regularly can be a great benefit for your family.

Eating together at the dinner table can be a great way to teach your child about the nutrition in their food. It is also an opportunity to try new cuisines with them and find healthy meals they love. Exercise shouldn't be forgotten, either. In my home, we take a daily walk around the neighborhood and then everyone pitches in to fix dinner when we get back. This helps my kids know that exercise is just as important as eating, plus it helps them work up an appetite!

The Importance of Physical Health

According to the Centers for Disease Control and Protection, 18.6% of children between the ages of six and 11 are obese. That's nearly one-fifth of our children suffering with weight issues before they are teenagers. It's a difficult issue to combat in our fast-paced world, and one parents hope they won't have to face, but it can all come down to family habits.

To keep your child from becoming part of this statistic, it is necessary for the entire family to be dedicated to eating healthy foods and keeping an active schedule. Routines such as eating a balanced breakfast every morning and going for walks or runs daily can help children learn to prioritize their health in the face of fast-food restaurants and junk food aisles. It also ensures they will get the nutrition they need to grow and develop at a healthy pace.

There are many benefits to eating healthy beyond forming good habits. When your child eats a balanced diet, it can help to stabilize their blood sugar and, thus, their energy levels. This means no more 2 p.m. tantrums after they have a sugary afternoon snack! Having these levels evened out can help their brains function more efficiently and their thought processes clearer. Even their moods can improve when you switch to a healthy diet because their food will work with their body instead of against it. Not to mention, without copious amounts of saturated fats and sugar, their weight will remain normal for their age.

Wholesome diets can even help people, especially our children, avoid developing chronic diseases such as diabetes, heart disease, or high blood pressure. We like to think nothing so serious could ever happen to our children, but if we aren't diligent about feeding them a variety of nutritious foods, it's a very real possibility.

Diets can't do it alone, though. Daily exercise is a healthy diet's perfect pair and a great way to spend all our child's extra energy. The CDC recommends that kids aged 6-17 get at least one hour of physical activity a day. Most children will do this through school during recess or P.E., but sometimes they aren't getting as much outside time as you might think. If your child still seems rambunctious when they get home from school, take them to the park or let them bounce around your backyard until they tire themselves out.

Despite benefits such as developing stamina and strength, very few children get the exercise they need just from school. Therefore, it's important to make sure your child gets exercise at home, even if you think they had enough at school. Any variety of things such as state testing, weather, or sick classmates can affect a school's recess time, and might lead to your child not getting to play outside at all one day.

If shifting your diet seems too intimidating, try thinking of it as a journey. You will need some trial and error in the kitchen to find the right path and what works for your family, but once you make it to the main road, it'll be an easy ride. You want to ensure that you are always fueling yourself to take the next step in your day, so you have to feed yourself the right way.

Breakfast is the key to the engine for your day. We've all heard the tropes about how breakfast is the most important meal of the day for our entire lives, and it's good enough to pass on to our kids. Focus on a breakfast complete with protein, clean fats, and lean carbs to fuel your child in the morning. This can be avocado toast with bacon or a sausage biscuit with coconut oil instead of butter. These food types will help to keep your child full and energized until lunch time.

Lunch can sometimes be tricky for parents because you often rely on their school to serve them a well-rounded meal. Still, you can use this as an opportunity to teach your child about making healthy choices whether they have options for their lunch. Sit down with them and go over the lunch menu to have them pick out which foods are the most nutritious. This can make it easier for them to pick healthy choices on their own when they are faced with a sea of options.

Some kids have metabolisms as fast as The Flash, however, and might still find their tummies rumbling before dinner time. If this sounds like your child, then be prepared to keep him or her away from the candy and chips by packing an alternative snack. You can send a bag of almonds and a stick of string cheese for them to enjoy if they need it and it won't cause their blood sugar to spike and crash like other snacks might.

The last step in your daily journey is dinner. When you plan this meal, remember to be aware of your child's activity levels during the day. If you have them play for an hour when they get home from school, you might need to serve dinner a little earlier because they've worked up an appetite. If they typically get all their exercise at school and have had a snack, you can usually wait a little longer to feed them. This meal is also the easiest to have all together as a family so everyone can connect over a wholesome meal.

If you're accustomed to a quick diet of take out and easy snacks, making this change can be difficult. Take the steps incrementally to ease your family into the new style of eating. Instead of throwing out all of your children's typical snacks, pick one snack to replace with a piece of fruit or a vegetable and over time work up to switching them all out. The thing you should focus on eliminating first is sugar, as it can have the most negative health effects. You don't have to ban it altogether, but start limiting how much your children can have and how much you include in the meals you cook. As you wean your family off the substance, they'll miss it less and less and you'll save yourself an all-out brawl over that pack of cookies.

How to Promote Healthy Choices

Ultimately, your child will follow your example so if you want them to make healthy choices you'll have to as well. Modeling this behavior can save you a lot of time and arguments when you want your child to eat his vegetables or forgo a popsicle. If you eat the foods you insist they try, your children are more likely to believe that it tastes good and give it a shot.

If you want to promote healthy habits, then promote the actions that go with them. Take your child with you to the grocery store and let them help you pick out the food for the week. You can take this opportunity to show them different fruits and vegetables and help them understand where their food comes from. It's also a great chance to let them have a say in what they eat for snacks; you can let them pick between two approved options, so they feel that they have a little more control over their lives.

Don't be afraid to get creative! I know that using the tried-and-true chicken casserole recipe will save you a ton of time in the kitchen, but your family has had it every night this week. Moving away from your comfort zone and trying new ingredients and cuisines can help to incorporate more foods into your diet and show your kids that new food is fun. The excitement of finding a new and great recipe is worth the extra 30 minutes you'll spend over the stove, I promise.

Choosing to eat healthy as a family is a commitment that every member should honor. You have enough on your plate without adding short-order cook to the list. Even if you have picky eaters, fixing everyone an identical plate of food can help tremendously in getting the family on board to change their diet. You don't have to force anyone to eat, but let them know that whatever you cook is what's for dinner and the choice to eat it is theirs.

There are countless times during the day that your child will tell you they're hungry. Very few of these times, I bet, will you believe them. This is why it can help to teach your child to look for his or her hunger cues, such as a growling tummy, or feeling tired. Even at a young age, it can be easy to succumb to eating out of boredom when snacks are plentiful and the pantry is always stocked, but if we can get our young children to keep a healthy relationship with food, then we drastically decrease the likelihood of them developing an emotional eating problem later in life.

Whether or not they are telling the truth, though, you can offer them a healthy snack. You want to make sure that you are reinforcing your child's natural ability to interpret their body's signals, such as hunger. So instead of making them wait until the next meal, let them discern if they really need food. If they wanted a treat and you offer them a nutritious snack instead, odds are their hunger will magically disappear anyway. You can also make sure to keep your child hydrated during the day or supplement snacks with dairy to keep their hunger at bay.

Encourage physical activity by making it a family event, just like dinner time. Instead of telling your child to go outside and play alone or with their siblings, you can get the whole family together for a walk to the park or a quick soccer game in the backyard. When you're a kid, it's much more fun to play with your whole family than by yourself and it can be a bonding experience for everyone, too.

Understanding the health benefits of certain foods can be tricky for adults, so it's reasonable to assume your child won't be interested on why their body prefers simple carbohydrates. Still, finding ways to explain nutrition to your child that they can understand can help them

How Children Succeed

appreciate why you encourage healthy eating. You can take time to explain how foods affect the body using emotions: too much sugar makes your body sad, but fruits and vegetables make your body happy. You can even share how certain foods make *you* feel and ask your child if any foods make them feel full, hyper, or yucky.

When you describe foods to your children, try to avoid labeling items as good or bad. It's important for young kids to understand that every food has a different place in their diet. Some might have large roles, and some might have minuscule roles, but every food belongs. To teach them this, you can color code foods in your home with the colors on a traffic light. They can eat as much as they want of foods labeled green; yellow foods they can have in moderation and have to ask before getting seconds; red foods are special treats and they need permission to eat them.

In hand with this exercise is an opportunity to teach your children about portions. As they learn which foods best support their bodies, they can also learn how to moderate their consumption, such as with yellow labeled foods. You can teach this lesson with a cup of rice. Let your child scoop the rice and see how small the grains are before pouring them into the water. Then, let them scoop out a bowl after it is cooked and notice how much bigger the grains got. You can explain that this is what happens to some food in their tummy, so they don't need to eat as much as they think they do to feel full.

When you cut out sugar, your whole family—yes, even you—will still crave sweets. The key to getting over this hump is to substitute your sweets with healthier options. Instead of giving your kids that fruit snack, give them actual fruit. Instead of eating that cookie, have a square of dark chocolate. These things can help satisfy the sweet tooth without having to cave into sugar.

CHAPTER 8

Become a Happier and Less Stressed Person Yourself

Being a mom is *tough*. I mean really tough. You are juggling multiple people's schedules, driving all over town, shoving sandwiches in backpacks, and praying that everyone's homework is done. Not to mention keeping up with your own career and somehow finding time to take a shower. The never-ending onslaught of tasks can bring extreme levels of stress that you are constantly pushing through to keep the train on its tracks.

I give you permission to stand still for ten seconds and take a deep breath. Feels pretty good doesn't it? Don't let yourself feel guilty for it, just enjoy the tiny release in your muscles when you exhale. Finding time to spend on yourself is nearly impossible as a parent, but it is necessary to maintain a healthy household. When a mom is stressed, everyone's stressed. Take opportunities during the day to cater to your own mental health so that you can be the cool, calm, and collected parent you aspire to be.

Catching Feelings

We all try to put on a brave face in front of our children. We don't want them to know that our boss was a jerk today or how our coworker dropped the ball on a huge project. We try so hard to hide our stress from them, so it doesn't burden their minds. Our children are much more perceptive than we give them credit for, though.

Children who grow up in families with a lot of conflict, not surprisingly, fair worse than children who grow up with a family that gets along. This is because, even if you don't notice, your children are picking up on those small moments where the stress wins. The moments when your anger leaks out or you become so overwhelmed you have to walk away. This perceptiveness is why some children benefit from having a single-parent family free of conflict than both parents who are always in conflict.

Adults are constantly handling stress from a barrage of different sources. Most of us are just trying to keep our heads above water. You might think if you can just keep the train moving, nothing will go wrong. The negative feelings you keep bottled up can leak into your routines, though. Your children might feel your tension as they rush to make it to school on time or you pick them up a little late because of rush hour traffic.

This is not a sign that you are a bad parent. This is a sign that you are a human being. If you talk to other mothers, you will see that everyone feels this way sometimes. Some people might even tell you of a story when they reacted inappropriately because they were so stressed. You are not alone in your struggle to make it all work, hold your tongue, or keep your temper. Stress is a natural part of life and one time or another, your child will be exposed to stressed out adults no matter how Zen their home is.

If you can identify your stress triggers, it can be much easier to cope with your feelings or avoid them altogether. Common triggers include time demands, money problems, career expectations, health concerns, and self-doubt. Nearly everyone has felt these pressures in their life at one point or another, but when they are constantly on our brains, it can create a lot of unwanted anxiety.

A stressful environment can even go so far as altering your child's gene. Abnormal stress in pregnant women has been linked to developmental problems in children such as anxiety, ADHD, and an increased risk to be on the autism spectrum. Being stressed out in your child's early years can even cause changes to their genome.

This shows that our children can be much more intuitive than we realize. When they see stress in us, they want to help fix the problem. They will do their best to understand the problem, but it will usually go over their heads. This can lead to them internalizing your stress and their frustration at not being able to help. They might even start acting out because they can't make sense of their feelings or yours.

Feeding off your emotions is sometimes referred to as emotional contagion, which is the idea that emotions can be passed along to people like an illness. When someone in the room feels angry or happy, most of the other people will follow suit and take on this emotion. This is what our children do when they see us acting stressed or upset, except they don't understand why they feel that way too.

How Children Succeed

Unlike your child, you have the ability to regulate your emotions and decide how to react to situations despite how you feel. There are two paths emotions can take between parent and child: the low road and the high road. The low road represents those snap decisions you make when you are mad or the bad word that slipped out while you were yelling. It's decisions that we know were inappropriate, but couldn't stop in the moment. The high road represents the positive moments; the times you take a step back, take a deep breath, and think before you speak or act. Children have this decision to make when they communicate with you, too, but as we all know they typically opt for the low road because they trouble regulating their emotions.

The contagion can work both ways. You've probably been in a situation where your child go so angry, they started wrecking their room or throwing their toys against the wall and you had the urge to throw toys too. This is because your child's anger is contagious; it triggered your own reaction to the situation, but you most likely were able to control those feelings and react in a better way.

This phenomenon might seem difficult to manage at first because none of us like feeling angry or annoyed. You can turn these moments around by using them as a chance to be empathetic with your child. Don't get mad because they are mad; try to understand what has upset them so much and start a conversation. Teaching your child the value of empathy and how to communicate his or her feelings can help both of you diffuse the stress in the situation.

Keeping Happy

With everything you deal with on a daily basis, it might seem impossible to limit your stress. Even when you feel guilty about putting your feelings on your child, it can feel like an inevitable aspect of being a parent. There are tons of quick and easy ways you can manage stress to create a happier environment in your home.

First and foremost, you can benefit from limiting your exposure to negative thoughts and media. These outlets put your brain in panic mode and can lead your thoughts to spiraling out of control before lunch. The news can often contain a slew of devastating stories and concerning reports that make you feel like the world is going to end. If you get these messages before you even start your day, good luck finding a positive mindset. Try nixing the morning report and waiting to catch the evening headlines so you can start your day in a calm headspace and maintain that relaxation throughout the day. You can even use the time you'd usually listen to the news to do some basic meditation or relaxation practices.

Waking up with negative pressures from social media or work emails can start a self-fulfilling doomsday prophecy in your mind. If the first thing you do is get sucked into these channels on your phone in the morning, you create a ball of anxiety that grows when you realize you're running late and ends up making you late because you can't think straight. It can follow all day, making you mess up a presentation you were nervous about or forget an important meeting.

Fortunately, the reverse can be just as effective. If you surround yourself with good news and positive thoughts in the morning, it can help you start the day feeling more relaxed and in control. You won't need to rush because you know where everything is, you won't be nervous about your presentation because you got to work on time, and you'll stop by the meeting to impress your boss. You can increase these happy feelings during the day by exchanging smiles and capitalizing on hugs. Positive vibes like to follow you around, too, so why not choose them as a daily companion?

You can also consider the future you, the one who is tired and sitting in traffic for an hour just to make it home from work. What are your needs? It can be hard for people to predict how they will feel in the future because our brains use only the present information. If you feel good, odds are you think you'll feel fine five hours from now, too.

Focus on your natural trend to anticipate your needs. If you know you always get hungry on the drive home and it makes you angry by the time you're home, pack a snack to eat in the car. Or if you're too tired to be kind in the mornings, go to bed earlier at night to get a little more sleep.

Give yourself more time during the day to accomplish things. If you are always rushing to make coffee and eat breakfast in the morning, start setting the coffee pot at night so it's ready when you wake up. Apply these creative solutions to your work life, too, so you can make your whole day easier. With all the time you've freed up, you can even pick up a hobby or two for yourself.

Our children can experience stress of their own, too. Between school and sports they might feel the pressure of having to perform at a high level all the time. It's important to know the signs of stress in children, such as irritability or moodiness, clinging to you (if they are young), and changes in sleeping or eating patterns. If you notice these in your child, ask if something is making them feel anxious or overwhelmed.

A conversation is the logical first step to addressing stress with your child, whether or not the source is at home. Make it a habit to ask about their day and how school was and listening while they answer. If they feel like they can talk to you without judgment, then they will likely let you know when things become too stressful for them to handle. Always let your child know that stress is normal before giving them your advice. In small children, you can listen for words like "worrying," "bothered," or "don't like" to indicate activities that might stress them out.

You do your best to portray positive messages to your children. Sometimes, though, the meaning can get lost in translation. Parents can get so worried about their child's future or if they will have a good life that their worry seeps into the edges of their messages. It's important to recognize this when it happens and adjust your message to include a healthier outlook.

Particularly in high school, you might be tempted to push your child to focus on the future, researching colleges, and setting themselves up to be the valedictorian in their class. This can put a lot of unnecessary pressure on them to succeed, though, and focuses on the results of their work instead of the effort they put in. Instead, teach your child how to live in the moment. So many of us get wrapped up in shaping our future that we forget to enjoy the time we have right now. Let your child take advantage of their youth and soak up every moment of high school that they can, without worrying about their future the whole four years. This can make them feel happier and perform better overall because they aren't fighting that internal pressure to succeed.

Parents can also let their own attitudes and stress influence the way they teach their children to deal with similar emotions. For example, if you've been dealing with sustained stress, you might give your child the "stress is inevitable" impression and show them they just have to put their head down and get through it. We need to be making efforts in the opposite direction. Teaching our children that it's okay to take time for themselves and that relaxing can help them not to get overloaded later in life when they have a job and a family of their own.

You can both practice relaxation methods together and, work on your stress levels as a family. Pick an exercise that feels comfortable for you, such as meditation, yoga, or deep breathing exercises, and start a routine to calm down each day and release stress. It can help your whole family learn how to decompress and not let stress control them, that way everyone has a happier and healthier mindset when they're together.

In our fast-paced world, it's almost default for us to get the idea that it is normal to be busy every second of every day. Don't feed into this idea. Don't pack your schedule full of back-to-back activities and commitments. Allow yourself to relax and take time for yourself and it will make you a more Zen kind of mom.

CHAPTER 9

Teach Problem-Solving Skills

Humans might look like innate problem solvers, but this is actually a learned skill, and a tough one at that. Despite its complexity, problem solving is an important activity for kids. It teaches them to think outside of the box and find ways to help themselves in difficult situations. It starts as soon as they can move around when they're babies; if they get too hot, they kick their blanket off or if they're hungry, they cry to get their mother's attention. These simple little actions are the seed of problem-solving abilities that will develop with them as they grow up.

We've all seen our children stumble across a problem and pause in pensive consideration. The difference is how we react. Some parents rush over and ask what's wrong and then fix the problem for their children, while others sit back and let their kids try to figure it out or bring it to their attention. The latter is letting their children develop their own style of problem solving by leaving them to find a solution. If you want your child to develop this useful habit, then let them ponder a little longer until they remedy the situation.

Why It's Important

Life comes with problems every day and not only when you're an adult. Kids face a variety of setbacks at school, sports practices, or with their friends. They may have trouble sitting still so they got moved to the back of the class where they don't like to sit. Or they struggle with a certain skill needed to play their favorite sport. Maybe their friend took their toy without asking and they aren't sure how to get it back. These problems require solutions that only they can come up with.

Most young kids haven't figured out how to deal with these problems on their own. They might end up avoiding the situation to keep from being confronted with an issue. This might lead to them falling behind in school or losing friendships. This can happen on the opposite end, too. Sometimes kids have trouble considering all the different ways they could solve a problem and act on their first instinct. This might mean hitting another child who cuts them in line because they don't know what else to do. To avoid these potentially harmful reactions to problems, kids need to learn how to solve their problems in a healthy way when they come across them.

Learning to address their problems on their own teaches a child how to maintain composure in the face of an emotional situation. Children lack the ability to regulate their emotions and can struggle to hold back anger or frustration when it bubbles to the surface. If they learn how to deal with these feelings and solve the problem, it builds their self-esteem and confidence, which makes them more likely to succeed next time.

Knowing how to solve their own problems can also help kids develop their personality. It can teach them patience and kindness while also allowing them to work their brain when they search for a creative solution. It can make them smarter and more agile in the face of adversity. This is because problem solving takes a certain level of higher order thinking that can be difficult for children at first. Making it through all the steps of solving an issue in their mind can be a lot to contain the first few times that they try. They also might not understand or be aware of all the options they have, but the more problems they tackle on their own the more solutions they will realize are available.

We have to let our children, even when they're young, find their own ways to solve the challenges they are faced with. If we swoop in and play Mr. Fix It every time something breaks or gets lost, then they will always wait for us to show up and make everything right again. They will miss out on the basic foundational skills of solving problems, which can make it harder for them to learn down the road.

When your child solves their own problems, they can start making better grades in school and even have improved behavior. This is because they have eliminated a situation that was causing them stress or negative emotions and freed up their mind to focus on the important things. It also gives them confidence to jump into new tasks and accept challenges with an open mind.

Problem solving is one of the many ingredients in the recipe for success. If you can teach your child to stick up for themselves and also create the right environment for healthy growth and development, then there will be nothing standing in their way on their journey to the top.

Children need a reliable environment and a steady routine to feel protected and safe from the outside world. This means having a stable home can have a huge impact on them. Kids' senses are especially attuned to the people around them, so if they sense problems that aren't being addressed or long-term issues, it might make it more difficult for them to find solutions in their own lives because of how stressful the problem might seem.

Staying in one location is also important so a child can develop a sense of belonging. If you move around every year or so, they might have trouble finding a place where they fit in and feel like the solution—not moving again—is out of their control. When they have one town and a group of friends that they can call their own it gives them the security and confidence to feel like they have control over the problems in their lives.

Successful kids who solve their own problems need plenty of opportunities to learn something new and to grow as a person. This means that as common problems arise, you can teach them how to solve them. If the tire on your car goes flat, show your child how to change it. If you are giving them an allowance, give them a large bill and teach them how to make a change. These little life skills will carry them through adulthood and make them feel competent and intelligent.

As they practice more of these skills, they will understand how they are useful and how they can apply to numerous occasions in life. Sheltering children from learning grown up skills only makes it harder for them when they are adults and need to know how to do these basic tasks. So don't trick yourself into thinking it's too early to teach them something because they are always ready to learn.

Children also get significant comfort from feeling connected to other people; it reinforces a sense of community and belonging. The more in touch they are with family members and friends, the more secure they feel in themselves and their abilities. This can help them not be scared to approach a problem in a unique way.

All kids, no matter their age, need to be encouraged to become successful. Children are always looking to adults for confirmation that what they did was a good thing or if they displayed any kind of talent. They can only find the things they are good at from securing that reassurance, and without it might doubt themselves and their abilities. If we want kids who aren't afraid to take care of themselves, we need to make sure we encourage their efforts and talents. Be optimistic when you talk about what they could accomplish or how they approached an issue. This will show them that the right way to handle a bad situation is with a positive attitude and outlook.

How to Teach Them

Your kids can learn everything they need about problem solving from you. All you have to do is create the right environment to let them handle issues as they arise and be there to support them through their trials and decisions. Not every solution will be a winner, but if you encourage them to keep going, they'll eventually find the right answer.

Encourage your child to be creative in everything they do. If they are accustomed to coming up with out-of-this-world ideas, then it won't be a far cry for them to find ingenious solutions to the problems they face during the day. It will feel natural to them to think their way around a situation and make it better.

Always be patient with your child when they are finding their solution. You might see the obvious solution to solve a problem, but let them find it on their own. Even if it takes them hours to put the pieces of a puzzle together, letting them figure it out on their own allows them to perfect their thinking processes and helps them make new connections in their mind.

How Children Succeed

Incorporate problem solving games into playtime to get them to flex those brain muscles without realizing the workout they're getting. Outdoor games such as hide-and-seek, capture the flag, or constructing a new toy can help to hone their investigative nature. Board games such as Connect Four or checkers can teach them to think about future problems and find ways to avoid them, which might even be more beneficial than solving problems in the moment.

The easiest way to teach your child problem-solving skills is to show them how you solve problems. Maybe they are watching you cook, and you accidentally add too much of one ingredient to the bowl. Explain your mistake and ask your child what they think you should do. You can work through the problem together and then explain why the solution you chose will work. Then let them watch you implement the solution so they can see if it was a good decision or needed more thought to solve the problem.

Even if they aren't watching you, you can still ask your kids to help you solve problems around the house. If the toilet is clogged, call your child into the bathroom and ask them how they think you could solve this problem. Let them stick around to see you plunge the toilet and see if it works or if it's a bigger task than you expected. If you have to call the plumber, you can explain that sometimes problems are too big for one person and you have to ask for help to solve it. This lets them know that if they try their best, and it still doesn't work, it's okay to ask someone for help.

Problems can be especially frustrating for children, so teach them how to field those emotions and work through them to find their solution. If they know that the strong feelings they have are only temporary, then it might make it easier for them to focus on the problem causing their anger. Teach them how to calm themselves down with deep breaths or by walking away from the issue until they feel ready to think about it again.

How Children Succeed

When you aren't around to help them make their way through the problem-solving process, you can teach your children five simple steps to remember. If they follow these steps on their own, they will have a surefire method to finding a peaceful solution to any problem.

First, they need to acknowledge their feelings. Ask them, do they feel angry, mad, or frustrated? If they can identify their emotions, then they should take a moment to acknowledge how they feel and calm down before attempting to solve their problem. You can teach them ways to do this like breathing exercises or taking a five-minute break until they feel more in control of themselves. Once their mind is clear and they feel more in control, they can return to the problem.

The next step is to identify the problem because it's hard to find a solution if you don't know what made you upset to begin with. They can assess their situation or go over the events that led them there to find where the fun broke down. Once they've found the problem, remind them it is theirs to solve and no one's fault. This can help them to not blame others for causing their distress.

Step three is brainstorming time. Your child can take a few minutes to think of as many ways to solve their problem as possible and make a list. This step isn't meant to designate which solution will work best, it's just a drawing board to get their creative juices flowing and see how many ways they could solve a problem.

In step four, your child will then consider their list and all the ways the solutions could be implemented. They will have to think through the things they came up with to determine if they are viable options. Have them consider what would happen if they tried a certain option; would it be safe to do on their own or will they ask an adult to help? They should also think about how the solution might make other people feel, especially if it is a group activity. Sometimes finding a way to fix something that seems good to your child might not be so great for their friend. Teach them that the best solution means everyone gets a little of what they want, and no one gets hurt or feels upset. This is the best way for them to remember that they need to use empathy and social skills even when they attempt to solve problems.

Now, they can move onto the last step in the process and try out the best solution. They've taken their time to consider each option and should be able to pick the best one. Keep in mind, though, that even something that seems perfect in theory still might not work in real life. If the first thing they try is a bust, let them know that it's okay, and it happens to everyone. All they have to do is move on to their next choice and keep trying different options until they find the right solution.

CHAPTER 10

Encourage Entrepreneurship

It used to be every kid's dream to open a lemonade stand on their block. We would beg our parents to buy us the supplies and show us how to make it and then we'd sit outside for hours hoping someone would come by and want to pay 25 cents for a glass. This was the entrepreneurial spirit. This teaches kids how the world works and how money works. It cements the idea that hard work equals profits and profits equals fun (at least until they start paying bills).

Encouraging entrepreneurship in your child helps them analyze the world around them and find problems they can solve. It gives them business savvy and sales experience that they carry into their first job and possibly their career. They might not start the next big tech company, but having a modest side business can give children the confidence to handle more of their life independently. Plus, if they can earn their own money you don't have to keep doling out $20s for the movies.

What They Can Learn

Promoting a child's entrepreneurial spirit can be one of the easiest parenting tasks. It might seem strange at first to explain the bitter truths of the world to your child, but they want to know. They're trying to figure things out and get in on the action. If you let them take their chances with a business idea, it can teach them how to adapt to change and demand and removes the fear associated with risk. It can be the best way to breed confidence and an outgoing personality.

With a business comes the need for all the skills you use at your job every day. Your child will have to learn self-discipline. If they're running a lemonade stand, for example, they'll have to resist drinking all of their product while they sit in the hot sun. They will also need to learn time management. If they want to sell fresh lemonade, then they need to see how long it takes them to make one pitcher before they spend their whole day juicing lemons and run out of time to sell it. Running a business also takes time out of your day, so they will have to balance their work activities with their school and sports commitments. Once they make a profit, though, they'll get to bask in the glow of that "I did it!" feeling.

Social skills are also a part of business and an entrepreneurial child can learn a lot through their venture. To sell something, they will have to interact with all kinds of people who are hopeful customers. They'll learn how to answer questions with authority, reassure people of quality, and encourage others to adjust their own resolve to make more sales. These aspects can all give your child practice looking for and interpreting non-verbal cues, as well as when to and when not to take no for an answer.

Business also gives children exposure to decision-making situations in a different way than at school or home because their money is on the line. At school they might have to decide if they want to split their lunch with a friend or eat it all, but in business they have to make sure that splitting that lunch wouldn't cost them money in the long run. It teaches them that decisions can often be based on value and gives them experience factoring money into their thinking process.

It also exposes them to a variety of problems they will face as an adult, such as disgruntled customers, lack of resources, or a declining market. Maybe Jimmy stopped by your kid's lemonade stand and expected his drink to be sweet, but it was tart. Now your child has to decide if Jimmy, who is upset, should get a refund or if it's his loss that he didn't like the flavor. Do they protect their bottom line or make it right with the customer? In another scenario your child might have run out of money to keep buying supplies for his or her stand because no one was buying their lemonade. They'll have to either work for more money another way or come up with a more lucrative venture.

Finally, and perhaps more importantly, running a business teaches your children how to earn money on their own. They don't have to ask you for handouts anymore because they've found their own avenue to generate cash. Earning money helps children to understand the value of a dollar and associate items with how much they cost.

How to Raise an Entrepreneur

Your child might not innately have the sales spirit, but there are some ways you can teach them about business without them having to start their own. Kids are always curious about what you do all day, so show them! If you can, bring your child to work with you for a few hours once or twice a month so they can see what an office looks like and how it runs. They will get a sense of what it is like to be an adult so that when they grow up and get their own job, they won't be startled by the structure and rules.

While they sit on the floor in your office, you can ask them to come up with a list of business ideas or companies they would be interested in working for. They might write down things they can sell from home or crazy made up companies with silly sales structures. Be sure to encourage diversity in their list so they know there are a wide variety of jobs that all match different personalities and work styles.

You can teach them the value of money by making them earn it at home. Allowances are popular among children and preteens, but giving children money that is not based on work can send the wrong message. Make a weekly chore list for your kids that you check off when they complete a chore. If they finish all of their chores for the week, then they get their allowance because they've earned it. Once they earn an allowance, they can also start paying for their own activities. This teaches them how to budget and reinforces the value of their work.

Aside from the value of money, your children should also learn the impact money can make on others. Make it a point to donate things—food, toys, or money—to a local charity or food bank during the year. Take your child with you when you go to drop these things off and let them take a tour of the facility. Learning what a difference their good fortune can make for others will help them be kind with their wealth.

Your child might seem interested in starting a business, but have trouble finding the right niche for them. Help them create a list of things they love to do and how they could market them. This could be crafts, cooking, or helpful services that others would enjoy. You can encourage them to create a marketing strategy so people know what they are selling and can contact them for more information. Learning to communicate with an audience is one of the key skills in business and in life.

When your child generates a steady income, from allowance or their business, open a bank account for them. Having exposure to how banking works at an early age can make them more confident about handling their money when they're an adult. Teach them how to check their account to see how much money is in it, and what they need to do to take money out. It also has the bonus of making your child feel like a grown-up, which comes with the best smile in the entire world.

Handling their own money can teach your child to be self-sufficient and running a business can teach them how to be an effective leader. Every good business is prone to expansion, and the bigger it gets the more friends your child will need in on the project. With all these people, though, they will have to keep everyone organized and on the same page with their business vision. It's how they will learn to communicate with others in a business setting and lead by example.

Entrepreneurism is all about swimming against the current and following your heart. It can show your child that being who they are is more profitable than following the crowd. If they trust their gut and follow their dreams, they might be able to create something bigger than they ever imagined. This success can show them that taking risks and doing scary things is sometimes all it takes to reach new heights.

Kids have little capital, so you might be tempted to act as an "investor" and cover the upfront costs of getting their business off the ground. Although this is a very generous offer and does occasionally happen in the real world, it's more likely they'd have to pay for things themselves. Recreate this scenario when they're young and begging to start a business by letting them earn the money they need to purchase supplies. It can give your child a confidence boost when their business takes off because they know they did it entirely on their own from start to finish.

Once the business is up and running, you will need to remind them to monitor their process and look for anything that might need adjusting. As their customer base grows, they might need to ramp up production or focus only on products that are generating the most money. Being able to adjust for the circumstances at hand can be a great skill to have both for your personal life and in future jobs.

If your child seems keen on starting a business, but nervous to take the plunge, there are a few things you can help them believe so they can succeed. The first is that all ideas are valid, so no matter what their business idea is, someone in the world will love and appreciate it. The second thing is that to make profits they will have to put in the hard work to make it happen. Lastly, let them know that creativity is key, and innovation makes people stand out. Help them think outside of the box and come up with creative solutions to common problems.

Each of your children's business ventures will end a different way, so the trick is to teach them how to come back from failure and find something new. If you can foster a high level of resiliency in your children, then they will never feel defeated or like there is no road to turn on. This is the trademark of any competent entrepreneur.

If you're struggling to come up with business ideas that your child could manage on their own, there are lots of options aside from the ever-classic lemonade stand. You could accompany your child selling something door-to-door in your neighborhood. Lots of schools and clubs require children to sell things like candy bars or raffle tickets for fundraisers. Let your child work on a sales pitch and practice it before going out to people's houses with you and trying to secure some sales. This also saves you from selling it all at your office.

Your child might be interested in starting a garden in the backyard. This is something you can turn into a business too! Let them learn how to grow their vegetables or flowers and then when the time comes, they can harvest their crop. If your plants were very healthy, you will likely end up with more than your family can eat. Set up a table in the driveway and let your child run their own little farmer's market selling the excess crop.

For older kids in middle and high school, tutoring can be a lucrative side business. Taking their talents and helping other people develop those skills also teaches your child the value of helping others. They can set up a schedule where they tutor their peers one-on-one at your home or the library, or they can teach small classes if multiple people are struggling in the same area. This business will also give them extra practice with their own studies and in time management and planning.

Babysitting turns into a great business for some children. Living in a neighborhood can be a particular advantage to this venture because they can put up flyers or start working with families you are familiar with. It teaches them how to be responsible and keep their word to others, while also giving them practical experience in how to care for others and themselves when adults are away.

Pet-related businesses can be all the rage for your little animal lover. They can focus on a variety of services such as dog walking, pet sitting, or helping to check in during the day while someone is at work. It gives them the exposure to animals they crave (without you needing to invest in a pet) and teaches them how to care for another living thing.

Lawn mowing businesses are popular in the summer, especially among teenage boys. These can get a little more complicated than other businesses because they need to make sure they have working equipment, know how to invoice customers, and work around the schedules of multiple people. It's a great way to learn the value of hard work and the basics of how to run a business.

Car washes are often used for fundraisers, but it can also be a simple service your child offers people in your town. They can set up a station in your driveway so customers can pull up and sit in their cars, or maybe opt to relax outside in a shaded area with free lemonade while your child cleans their car. This can teach them how to adapt to customer feedback to make sure their customer are always happy.

CHAPTER 11

Physical Confidence

Not every child will be a sports star, but they can all feel confident in their own physical abilities. When I was a kid, I was a total klutz, but my parents still let me try out for any sport I wanted to play. My eight-year-old child is the same way; she trips over her own two feet, but is bound and determined to play soccer every fall. If your children have similar attitudes, encourage that gumption! The more they go outside and work their muscles the more confident they become in their own abilities.

You can run around the park with your child, set up outdoor playdates, or enroll them in team sports to get their blood pumping and their bodies moving. There's no right way to get exercise, as long as they are working up a sweat and having fun. The more they practice certain activities, such as climbing trees or the monkey bars, the better they will get. This reinforces the lesson that they can do anything they set their mind to. So, if you're looking to raise confident, trail-blazing people, let them play!

Physical Activity

We discussed the importance of physical activity in chapter seven when we looked at how to raise healthy kids. Being active can contribute to more than just physical health, though. I can also help you teach your child to become more physically confident by exposing them to opportunities to try new feats of strength and cunning.

Physical confidence is your child's belief in their own abilities. For example, if your clumsy child is physically confident, they'll believe that they can still master baseball with enough practice. If they aren't, they might be afraid to try sports that require specific skills. You want your child to feel physically confident, so they are willing to learn new things and try new activities.

Exercise helps children excel in all areas of their lives. Active kids typically do better in school and have healthy relationships with their friends. They also are usually better behaved than other children who may not have had the opportunity to expend their energy. Physical confidence can even show improved mental health in all children. Having this confidence doesn't mean a child has to be lean and fit, either; overweight or bullied children can also find power in exercise to help them overcome their personal struggles.

It also goes beyond just being active. Kids who are physically confident are comfortable in their own skin and with different physical activities, so they are much less likely to be intimidated by something new. They tackle challenges with energy and enthusiasm because they feel secure in their ability to handle anything. Even though they are aware of their limits, they have also developed enough mental toughness to power through tough moments and come out on the other side, such as climbing a rope in P.E. or being tackled in football for the first time.

Your child doesn't have to play sports to develop physical confidence. They can develop these feelings in your own backyard or neighborhood park, as long as they are given the opportunity to play every day. Once they know that they can accomplish anything they set their mind to, it can make any exercise much more enjoyable and rewarding.

Like every other skill, if you want your child to enjoy the outdoors you have to model that passion for exercise. This is not to say you need to join a gym and become a bodybuilder because who has time for that? All you need to do is show your child that physical activities can be fun! Take them to a soccer field and kick a ball around with them or to the basketball courts to shoot hoops. You can even walk around the track at your local high school and see how fast they can run 50 or 100 meters. If being active is part of their daily life, then it won't seem like a difficult and scary thing.

At some point, your child might realize that the sport or activity they're involved in just isn't for them. In this situation, let them quit. Explain that they will have to finish the season and honor the commitment they made to the team, but next year they don't have to play if they don't want to. With this agreement, however, your child should also pick something to replace that sport. It can be anything they are interested in doing that has a physical element to it. This way they can try anything they might be interested in and learn what they love to do and what they'd rather not do.

The new activity your child chooses might be an off-the-wall idea, like pole vaulting or the trapeze. Both will probably be a little scary for both of you.

How Children Succeed

You might only think about how far they are from the ground if they fall, and they might not realize how high they are until they're in the air. Despite these fears, support their interests. Let them try it out and reassure them that it's normal to be afraid at first and they'll get used to the feeling as they practice. This is how they learn that even things that seem scary and impossible can be accomplished with a little perseverance.

Help your children set physical goals for themselves. Maybe your son loves to read books about famous tennis players; you could ask him if he'd like to try to learn tennis. You can get rackets and balls and take him out to a tennis court at the park and let him practice playing the game. (You don't have to be good at the sport, just learn with him!) He might decide he wants to try out for the local tennis league. You can help him practice and set goals such as five successful serves in a row or ten returns on one round so he feels confident when the try-outs come.

Establishing Confidence

Self-confidence is a crucial part of children's lives. It's what gives them the fuel to make friends, join teams, and start new schools. Without it, they would have trouble adjusting to their ever-changing world and facing all the challenges life throws at them. There are a few things you can do to help your child develop the confidence they need to succeed.

Self-confidence is the precursor to physical confidence, and it starts to develop when your child is a baby. The easiest way to foster confidence at young ages is to establish a routine for them. Make sure they wake up, eat their meals, and go to bed at the same time. Pack their days with the same activities so they know what to expect when they wake up. This helps children feel safe, secure, and in control of their environment, which helps them to feel comfortable exploring and learning new things.

How Children Succeed

Having plenty of time to play helps children discover themselves and learn important social skills. Babies can play with toys or other small children and as they get older, you can go to playgrounds or parks and let them have fun as long as they want. Kids are great at making impromptu friends and public places offer a natural arena to work together with strangers or start a fun game with a new group of people. This can help your child determine if they prefer to be the leader or the follower in a group and how to establish themselves as either.

In groups, and in life, problems will inevitably arise. You can teach your children to solve these on their own to further develop their confidence and independence. Perhaps your daughter is on a soccer team, but some of her teammates refuse to pass her the ball during a game or at practice. You can see she is upset, so you sit down and ask her to find the root of the problem: why won't the girls pass her the ball? When she discovers the answer, she can find a solution such as talking to the girls and telling them that their behavior is hurting her feelings.

Responsibilities at home can also help children develop confidence when they know that they can help you keep the house running smoothly. Sometimes kids will even want to help with outdoor chores, such as cutting grass or pulling weeds. These are great tasks to help them build their physical confidence because they require hard work and diligent effort that kids don't usually expect going into it. Once they finish weeding your entire flower bed or cutting all the grass, they will undoubtedly be very proud of their work.

We like to do our best to treat our children equally, but the truth is there are a lot of differences in raising a girl versus raising a boy. Most efforts we read or hear about in today's world are aimed at girls. We do our best to keep them from feeling pressured by beauty or lifestyle stereotypes in society and to celebrate their natural beauty and personalities. This can make some of us forget, however, that boys face similar stereotypes and need just as much nurturing to feel secure.

Things can be difficult for boys from the get-go. Daycare and school is typically tough for young boys because they lack the impulse control that girls of the same age have because their brains develop at a different rate. This can mean they get in trouble more often or are fussed at constantly during the day. To keep their confidence high, be sure to praise their good behavior so they don't feel like they are always in trouble. If there's anything particular they're struggling with in school, you can encourage them to work on it at home to develop those skills.

Boys can also feel like they are constantly in competition with other boys, whether it's who's the fastest or tallest or biggest or strongest. Combatting this feeling that they need to be the best can be easy, but needs to be consistent. Point out the differences in the boys your son meets and let him know that just because they are different, doesn't make them better or worse. Explain that everyone has different skills and talents and they need to work together to be the best team they can be. If you are watching a television show or movie and you see the characters depicting stereotypes, be sure to point out it doesn't apply to all boys. You can say, "Wow, he's good at sports, but not all boys are, huh?"

Our society also puts a lot of pressure on boys to be tough and "buck up" when they start to feel sad or hurt. People reinforce the idea that boys shouldn't cry, but this can lead to them becoming out of touch with their feelings as they grow. If your son has a bad day or falls and scrapes his knee, let him cry if he needs to and offer some comfort like a hug or a kiss. You can ask him to tell you how he's feeling, so he starts to learn how to express his feelings instead of shoving them down. Try to find men that model this behavior and let them be an example for your son to reinforce that they can be a good man and have feelings.

How Children Succeed

When we foster self-confidence and teach our children the value of exercise, we will breed physically confident youngsters. This can teach them to be good leaders in a variety of different settings, especially if we can step in and reinforce the correct behaviors and habits.

First, you can encourage team sports or group activities to get your child accustomed to working with others. This gives them an opportunity to learn the unique communication style and skills they need to succeed in a group and also where they are most comfortable fitting in. They might get to be a team captain and have to learn what it takes to lead other people to victory.

Sometimes taking the gold means making compromises, and to do that your child will have to be a skilled negotiator. Negotiating can play a huge role in adult life: negotiating your salary, buying a car, buying a house. It's a skill every adult needs and uses. Kids, however, are used to the finite answers of yes and no. As difficult as it can make your life, teaching your children to negotiate instead of taking these two words as the end all, can help them later down the road. Instead of answering their request for a second cupcake with "no," offer something else like a glass of water and then work with your child to find an acceptable compromise.

Leadership roles require your children to confidently communicate their needs and ideas, which can be scary when you're young. Give your children opportunities to practice communicating with other people, such as ordering their own food in a restaurant or telling the hairdresser what kind of haircut they want. When we act as a buffer between our child and other adults, it can make them feel like they aren't able to communicate their needs on their own.

Good leaders are hard workers, so encourage your child's natural drive to work. You can let them pick up extra chores around the house to earn extra money, or let them start their own business, or even (if they're old enough) let them apply to jobs around town. All these suggestions give them an opportunity to develop job skills that they will need one day in the real world. The more familiar they are with how to earn a living, the easier it will be when they grow up and go out on their own.

CHAPTER 12

Kids' Social Skills

Odds are your children have a larger friend circle than you do, which is a good thing! Kids need plenty of social interaction to learn how to relate to others and make friends. My oldest daughter always starts her interactions the same way: She sticks out her little hand and introduces herself to every person in the room she doesn't know. The first person to strike up a conversation she is interested in gets to be the lucky winner for the next half an hour because she will tell them all about her interests and hobbies and siblings and

How Children Succeed

anything else she can think of.

Not all kids are this precocious. Some children prefer to hang back and might feel a little intimidated in social situations, even with their peers. Being introverted is perfectly fine, but you want to make sure your child isn't afraid of interaction. Helping them overcome these fears can help keep them from developing social anxiety when they get older and make them more comfortable around a diverse group of people. Keep an eye out for how your child acts in a group of friends or around strangers to assess if you need to give them a little extra encouragement or coaching about how to relate to others.

What to Look For

Every age group of children has different social abilities. You wouldn't expect your two-year-old to strike up a conversation with someone, just like you would expect your six-year-old to be polite when speaking to an adult. There are certain stages of development kids go through that gradually increase their skills when interacting with others. You can make sure they are reaching the appropriate milestones as they grow to help them stay on track to develop healthy relationships and great social skills.

Young toddlers who are two or three years old are typically old enough to look for attention from others. This might be the baby in the grocery store who stares at you until you smile at them, or the little girl who waves at you on the sidewalk. At this age, your child should be starting to say "hi" and "bye" to people, too. They should be able to look at the person who is speaking, laugh when something silly happens, and take turns speaking.

When your child approaches or reaches age four, they should develop some new skills. At this age, your child should recognize that they need to take turns when they play with others and share their toys. They will usually play with their stuffed animals or dolls as if they are real and assign them emotions or personalities. They should now also be able to initiate a conversation using their own words or introducing themselves to others.

Four and five-year-olds will build on these skills by showing more cooperation with their friends and adults. They will also start asserting themselves in social situations by using direct requests such as "Stop." This is usually the age when children will tell on each other the most, too. Your child might even shift their imaginary play to pretending to be you or your spouse by putting on your shoes or clothes. They might even play mom or dad when playing house with their friends.

As your child gets closer to six years old, they will learn and understand basic manners, such as saying please, thank you, and I'm sorry. This is the age when they develop a deeper understanding of language such as what bad words are and why they shouldn't say them. Unfortunately for parents, this is also the age where they get good at bargaining. Remember that negotiation skill we mentioned in the last chapter? Your five or six-year-old will be a master at capitalizing on it. In addition to these, your child might also start playing competitively and understand what it is to be a good sport and play fair.

When your child is about seven years old, they should be able to empathize with other people and events. If they see someone who is sad, they might feel sad, too. They should also use their posture and gestures to communicate, incorporating nonverbal cues in their vocabulary. They typically are much better at sharing, waiting their turn, and not blaming others for their mistakes or losses. This age likes to joke and laugh with their friends, being more open to others' opinions, and finding agreeable compromises. They can understand the difference between right and wrong, but might not take direction well as they try to find where they fit in the world.

Keep in mind that all children develop at a different pace, and your child might acquire some of these skills a little earlier or later than the ranges I've mentioned here. It's nothing to be worried about unless they are not developing the skills at all.

Some children are not as social as others and might prefer more time by themselves reading books or playing along. This is perfectly normal and probably indicates you just have a more introverted kid. It's important to distinguish the difference between them choosing to be alone and them being excluded. If they are alone because they are having trouble making friends, then it might be time to step in and assess the situation. Your child might have trouble communicating with others or reading the social cues that gives them hints on how to behave in a group.

You might notice your child having awkward interactions with other kids on the playground or at school. We all have awkward encounters from time to time, but if this is happening consistently, your child might be missing some skills they need to interact with others. They might continue talking when the other child wants to leave, or not waiting their turn to speak in a group. These can both be interpreted as strange or rude behavior, even by children, so taking the time to discuss them with your child can teach them why they have trouble making friends.

Children can face other social challenges too. Some kids might talk too much or not enough when they get nervous around people. This can make it difficult for others to hold a conversation with them. They might also struggle to identify sarcasm and not realize when children don't want to be around them or why. Sometimes they can struggle with finding the right things to talk about and end up sharing inappropriate information with others, making the group uncomfortable. Some kids can also struggle to read facial cues or body language and not be able to respond appropriately to the feelings the other person is conveying. If they are teased or struggle enough with social interactions, then your child might even withdraw from conversations and keep to themselves so he or she doesn't feel embarrassed or confused.

These challenges can make it difficult for children to develop a circle of friends or to connect with their family or teachers. It might make them feel isolated or different from everyone else, which can cause them to shy away from asking for help or addressing the problem. Sometimes feeling like an outsider can create a strong need for belonging that they have trouble filling without help.

A variety of different factors can affect your child's social skills. They might have issues with self-control that makes it difficult for them to stop talking even when someone is finished with the conversation. There could even be mental health issues or stress at home that is making the child feel like they need to seek affection elsewhere, but the skills to make friends were never demonstrated for them. In multicultural communities, language barriers can be a difficult thing for children to overcome. They might not know how to express themselves in another language and so they are limited in their ability to communicate with other kids. Even learning disabilities such as ADHD can impact a child's ability to have a successful conversation.

Teaching Social Skills

If you notice your child lacking in certain social skills, make it a point to explain different aspects of social interaction to them. Breaking down the different aspects of a conversation can help them understand what they are doing wrong or why they feel uncomfortable. For example, if your child talks too much, you can teach them about facial cues and body language so they can start practicing being respectful of nonverbal communication. You can even go over things such as personal space and taking turns speaking, depending on what areas your child needs help with.

Empathy is possibly the most important social skill, no matter how old you are. This is how we relate to others and have meaningful relationships. To help teach your child about empathy, start asking them if they can guess how other people feel. This can be in the grocery store, on the playground, or while watching television or reading a book. Point out people's facial expressions to your child so they can learn what to look for if he or she thinks someone is sad, mad, or happy. Understanding the other person's emotions can make it easier for your child to interact with a friend.

Role playing a conversation can help you show your child where they are going wrong in their interpersonal interactions. You can teach them how to wait for their turn to speak, how to listen to someone else, and how to include someone in a conversation. If you notice them doing something specifically wrong when they talk to their friends, then you can address that issue directly in the role playing. Start the conversation like normal and stop to show them why what they just did can be troubling. Then offer a solution on how to alter their behavior to get better results when they talk to their friends.

Basic manners are another key aspect of having a successful conversation. If your child is reluctant to say please and thank you or apologize when they've hurt someone's feelings, then it will be difficult for them to make friends. Enforcing the necessity of using these words at home will make them a habit for your child when they are in an unsupervised situation. If they know that to be friends with someone they have to say please and ask to share a toy instead of just grabbing it out of their hands, then they will continue to implement this on their own in an effort to make more friends and have an enjoyable play time.

One of the best ways to let your child practice their skills is to give them plenty of opportunities to be social. The more they are exposed to other kids, the more likely they are to learn the necessary skills on their own. This comes from feedback from their friends telling them to be nice or asking if they can please share. They will learn to model the behavior of the people they want to be around. Just make sure you are also respecting your child's social boundaries. As mentioned before, not all kids are extroverts, so if your child seems to be tired of playing with others, it's okay to take them home and allow them some alone time to unwind.

If you want to employ some regular activities to help your child develop social skills, you can first pick the skill you want to develop and then make a game out of it. If you are looking to develop more subtle skills such as recognizing nonverbal cues, you can use television shows to help show them to your child. Pick one of their favorite shows and watch an episode with the sound turned off. Throughout the show, you can ask your child how they think a character feels based on their facial expressions and posture. After your child guesses a few, go back and watch the scene with the sound on to see how many emotions they guessed correctly.

To help your child learn about tone of voice, you can record yourself saying the same sentence but with different levels of emotion. You might say it once as if you're mad, sad, then as if you're excited. Have your child listen to the recordings and guess how you felt for each rendition of the sentence. You can add an extra step to this game by asking them how they would respond if one of their friends sounded like this, which teaches empathy as well.

Your child might have trouble paying attention when others are talking, so you can play a game in which listening is key. You can say three sentences, two of which are related, and one is not. Then, your child has to pick the sentence that isn't related to the other two. This helps them to pay attention when someone is talking and learn to listen for certain things in someone's story or instructions.

There are even games that can help your child maintain eye contact with others, which can especially be a problem with kids who have ADHD or are on the autism spectrum. Play silly games that have you stick things on your forehead, such as words that your child has to act out or make you guess. This way their focus will be on your forehead, which isn't quite your eyes, but is in the right direction. You can even use an old-fashioned staring contest to get them to practice making eye contact. Looking someone in the eye can be intimidating even for adults, but if you can turn it into a game, even the shyest of kids will have fun developing the skill.

CONCLUSION

Raising successful children can be an easy task if you have all the right tools and know how to encourage positive behavior. Hopefully, you've been able to implement some or all of these parenting techniques in your home. I know some of them can be a big adjustment, but making the effort makes a difference, so kudos to you for taking the leap! Maybe you're already seeing results from particular chapters and realizing that these are the 12 best tips to raise successful kids.

If you haven't started implementing these changes in your home, my advice is to start right away. The sooner you set up these new rules, the easier it is for your children to adjust and accept it as the new normal. Plus, it can take a lot of pressure off you when you establish chores and responsibilities as a routine instead of something you ask for every now and then.

Remember that consistency is key. If you decide that your child needs to clean their room every Saturday, then make sure it happens every Saturday regardless of circumstance. It's easy to let one weekend slide because your son played in a baseball tournament all day, but that leads to every excuse feeling sufficient to let them have a pass. Your child has much more energy than you think and picking up their clothes or making their bed won't be their undoing at the end of a long day outside.

A considerable amount of future success depends on academic success, especially in high school and college. So, you shouldn't overlook teaching them reading and math or how to study and manage their own time. I know how strange it can feel to sneak in mathematic principles while your child is playing. I also know how frustrating it can be, reading to a child who does not want to sit still. I can tell you, though, that it is worth the discomfort. I've seen my oldest child flourish in school and my younger two take on new subjects with a surety I never had in school. This determination to master new skills will follow your children into adulthood and translate into their careers.

Teaching our children to live healthy lives can help them feel physically and mentally well. We've all heard (and maybe experienced) the "Freshman 15" in college, referring to the extra weight most new adults gain when they move out of their parents' home. Some people spend the rest of their lives struggling with weight loss and self-esteem. If you can make eating healthy a normal part of your child's life, then eating a balanced diet as an adult will come naturally to them. Physical fitness contributes to mental health and can help your child feel capable and in control.

As I'm sure you noticed, a lot of the skills

necessary to create lifelong habits are also great ways to instill confidence within your child. Confidence gives children an outgoing spirit and the knowledge that they can accomplish anything they set their minds to. It can make them more resilient, determined, and creative than you could ever dream. It also helps them not to be afraid of challenges or changes in their lives. Teaching them things such as that failure is okay, your effort is what's important, how to develop their physical abilities, and how to solve problems on their own can show them they are stronger than they believe.

So there you have it, all the tried-and-true ways to raise successful children, as promised. You can use the specific activities and techniques I described to teach the skills, or find unique ways to shake them up to better fit your family. The more you practice, the better your children will become, and you can watch them take charge of their lives, becoming more responsible and independent.

If you take anything away from this book, please let it be this message: you are a great parent! Just taking the time to read these tips shows that you are invested in your child's success and willing to go the extra mile to prepare them for adulthood. So no matter how hard things get or how crazy your schedule is, remember that you are great at raising your kids.

Thank you!

Thank you so much for reading this book! I hope you liked it! As you know, I love hearing back from anyone who read my books to know how I did and know if I helped one more person. I would really appreciate it if you could please leave me a review and let me know what your thoughts are on this book! Thank you very much and good luck in your new journey!

REFERENCES

Anderson, J. (2015). Parents: Let Your Kids Fail. You'll Be Doing Them a Favor. Retrieved from https://qz.com/527652/parents-let-your-kids-fail-youll-be-doing-them-a-favor/

Arky, B. (n.d.). How to Build Boys' Self-Confidence. Retrieved from https://childmind.org/article/how-to-build-boys-self-confidence/

Bates, A. (2012). Important Math Skills in Early Childhood. Retrieved from https://education.cu-portland.edu/blog/classroom-resources/important-math-skills-early-childhood-educators-should-teach/

Booth, S. (n.d.). Teaching Kids to Eat Healthy. Retrieved from https://www.webmd.com/parenting/guide/food-smart-kids#1

Building Strong Family Relationships. (n.d.). Retrieved from https://www.udel.edu/canr/cooperative-extension/fact-sheets/building-strong-family-relationships/

Cully, C. (2014). How Parents Can Help Children Deal with Stress. Retrieved from https://www.parenttoolkit.com/health-and-wellness/news/stress/how-parents-can-help-children-deal-with-stress

Dell'Anotonia, K. (2018). Happy Children Do Chores. Retrieved from https://www.nytimes.com/2018/08/18/opinion/sunday/children-chores-parenting.html

Derhally, L. (2016). The Importance of Childhood Friendships, and How to Nurture Them. Retrieved from https://www.washingtonpost.com/news/parenting/wp/2016/07/25/the-importance-of-childhood-friendships-and-how-to-nurture-them/?noredirect=on

Dewar, G. (2016). Parenting Stress: 10 Evidence-Based Tips for Making Life Better. Retrieved from https://www.parentingscience.com/parenting-stress-evidence-based-tips.html

Dockterman, D. (2017). Turning High Expectations into Success. Retrieved from https://www.gse.harvard.edu/news/uk/17/08/turning-high-expectations-success

Doucleff, M. (2018). How to Get Your Kids to Do Chores (Without Resenting It). Retrieved from https://www.npr.org/sections/goatsandsoda/2018/06/09/616928895/how-to-get-your-kids-to-do-chores-without-resenting-it

Five-Step Problem Solving for Young Children. (n.d.). Retrieved from https://heartmindonline.org/resources/5-step-problem-solving-for-young-children

Five Ways to Set High Expectations Without High Pressure. (n.d.). Retrieved from https://www.melbournechildpsychology.com.au/blog/5-ways-to-set-high-expectations-without-high-pressure/

Gillett, R., & De Luce, I. (2019). Science Says Parents of Successful Kids Have These 23 Things In Common. Retrieved from https://www.businessinsider.com/how-parents-set-their-kids-up-for-success-2016-4

Gordon, B. (2018). Five Ways to Help Kids Develop Healthy Habits. Retrieved from https://www.eatright.org/health/weight-loss/overweight-and-obesity/5-ways-to-help-kids-develop-healthy-habits

Griffin, T. (2019). How to Improve Social Skills in Children. Retrieved from https://www.wikihow.com/Improve-Social-Skills-in-Children

Hathaway, E. (n.d.). How to Set Consistent Expectations to Improve Student Behavior. Retrieved from https://www.kickboardforschools.com/blog/post/the-value-of-consistent-expectations

Heitler, S. (2017). Chores: Secrets to Winning the Parent-Kids Chore-Wars. Retrieved from https://www.psychologytoday.com/us/blog/resolution-not-conflict/201707/chores-secrets-winning-the-parent-kids-chore-wars

Help Your Child Develop Early Math Skills. (n.d.). Retrieved from https://www.zerotothree.org/resources/299-help-your-child-develop-early-math-skills

Holecko, C. (2019). Seven Ways to Raise a Physically Confident Child. Retrieved from https://www.verywellfamily.com/ways-to-increase-physical-confidence-4078456

Hollman, L. (2017). Emotional Contagion: Catching Your Child's Feelings When You Use Parental Intelligence. Retrieved from https://www.huffpost.com/entry/emotional-contagion-catch_b_8540386

Homme, M. (n.d.). Five Things Every Child Needs to Be Successful in Life. Retrieved from https://www.lifehack.org/520358/5-things-every-child-needs-successful-life

Hurley, K. (2017). How Parental Stress Negatively Affects Kids. Retrieved from https://health.usnews.com/wellness/for-parents/articles/2017-04-21/how-parental-stress-negatively-affects-kids

Improving Kids' Social Skills. (n.d.). Retrieved from https://www.parents.com/kids/development/social/improving-kids-social-skills/

Ingram, C. (2007). Let Your Kids Fail. Retrieved from https://www.focusonthefamily.com/parenting/let-your-kids-fail/

Kaplana, M. (2019). Parent-Child Relationship: Why Is It Important and How to Build It. Retrieved from https://www.momjunction.com/articles/helpful-tips-to-strengthen-parent-child-bonding_0079667/#gref

Lavis, P. (2016). Why Relationships Are So Important for Children and Young People. Retrieved from https://www.mentalhealth.org.uk/blog/why-relationships-are-so-important-children-and-young-people

Lehman, J. (n.d.). Why You Should Let Your Child Fail: The Benefits of Natural Consequences. Retrieved from https://www.empoweringparents.com/art

icle/why-you-should-let-your-child-fail-the-benefits-of-natural-consequences/

Loh, A. (n.d.). Teaching Problem Solving Skills to Children. Retrieved from http://www.brainy-child.com/articles/teach-problem-solving-skills.shtml

Maniyamkott, M. (2017). Why You Should Encourage Entrepreneurship Among Kids. Retrieved from https://yourstory.com/2017/06/entrepreneurship-among-children

Morin, A. (n.d.). Growth Mindset: What You Need to Know. Retrieved from https://www.understood.org/en/friends-feelings/empowering-your-child/building-on-strengths/growth-mindset

Morin, A. (2019). How to Teach Kids Problem-Solving Skills. Retrieved from https://www.verywellfamily.com/teach-kids-problem-solving-skills-1095015

Morin, A. (2019). How to Use Praise to Encourage Good Behaviors. Retrieved from https://www.verywellfamily.com/how-to-use-praise-to-promote-good-behavior-1094892

Morin, A. (2019). The Importance of Chores for Kids. Retrieved from https://www.verywellfamily.com/the-importance-of-chores-for-kids-1095018

National Center for Health Statistics. (n.d.). Retrieved from https://www.cdc.gov/nchs/fastats/child-health.htm

Nutrition Tips for Kids. (n.d.). Retrieved from https://familydoctor.org/nutrition-tips-for-kids/

Ortillan, G. (2017). Standards vs. Expectations: Why You Need to Know the Difference in the Workplace. Retrieved from https://medium.com/@gilianortillan/https-medium-com-gilianortillan-standards-vs-expectations-why-you-need-to-know-the-difference-4fad66231772

Passing Healthy Habits onto Your Children. (n.d.). Retrieved from https://familydoctor.org/kids-passing-on-healthy-habits-to-your-children/

Pellissier, H. (2018). Why Early Math Is Just as Important as Early Reading. Retrieved from https://www.greatschools.org/gk/articles/early-math-equals-future-success/

Physical Activity Facts. (n.d.). Retrieved from https://www.cdc.gov/healthyschools/physicalactivity/facts.htm

Pinola, M. (2014). How Can I Help My Kids Develop Better Social Skills? Retrieved from https://lifehacker.com/how-can-i-help-my-kids-develop-better-social-skills-1557575829

Rampton, J. (2015). Fifteen Tips for Instilling Leadership Skills in Children. Retrieved from https://www.entrepreneur.com/article/241619

Responsibility and Chores. (n.d.). Retrieved from https://centerforparentingeducation.org/library-of-articles/responsibility-and-chores/part-i-benefits-of-chores/#struggle

Rippel, M. (n.d.). How to Motivate Your Child to Read. Retrieved from https://blog.allaboutlearningpress.com/motivating-kids-to-read/

Rutzler, S. (2017). Why You Should Teach Math at an Early Age. Retrieved from https://www.mathgenie.com/blog/why-you-should-teach-math-at-an-early-age

Scheff, S. (2012). Fifteen Ways Parents Can Promote Entrepreneurship. Retrieved from http://www.suescheffblog.com/15-ways-parents-can-promote-entrepreneurship/

Seppala, E. (2017). A Leading Happiness Researcher Says We're Giving Our Kids Bad Advice About How to Succeed in Life. Retrieved from https://qz.com/1021749/a-leading-happiness-researcher-says-were-giving-our-kids-bad-advice-about-how-to-succeed-in-life/

Sevier, S. (2017). Five Ways to Help Kids Build Healthy Relationships. Retrieved from https://www.parenttoolkit.com/social-and-emotional-development/news/relationships/5-ways-to-help-kids-build-healthy-relationships

Should I Let My Kids Fail? 5 Tips to Help Kids Face Failure. (n.d.). Retrieved from https://www.positiveparentingsolutions.com/parenting/should-i-let-my-kids-fail

Simmons, R. (2015). Before You Let Your Child Fail, Read This. Retrieved from https://www.huffpost.com/entry/before-you-let-your-child-fail-read-this_b_8005866

Six Ways to Improve Your Child's Social Skills. (n.d.). Retrieved from https://blog.brainbalancecenters.com/2017/06/6-ways-improve-childs-social-skills

Smith. S. (n.d.). Try These 10 Mindful Phrases to Effectively Praise Your Kids. Retrieved from https://www.mother.ly/child/try-these-10-mindful-phrases-to-effectively-praise-your-kids

Statistics About Diabetes. (n.d.). Retrieved from https://www.diabetes.org/resources/statistics/statistics-about-diabetes

Stuart, A. (n.d.). When Should Kids Learn to Read, Write, and Do Math? Retrieved from webmd.com/parenting/features/when-should-kids-learn-read-write-math#

Sundem, G. (2016). Why Is Your Child Good (Or Bad...) at Both Math and Reading? Retrieved from https://www.psychologytoday.com/us/bl

og/brain-trust/201602/why-is-your-child-good-or-bad-both-math-and-reading

Ten Benefits of Reading. (n.d.). Retrieved from https://www.cameverlands.org.uk/10-benefits-of-readåing/

Ten Tips: Be a Healthy Role Model for Children. (n.d.). Retrieved from https://www.choosemyplate.gov/ten-tips-be-a-healthy-role-model

Ten Tips on How to Build Confidence in Kids. (2019). Retrieved from https://www.workingmother.com/content/10-tips-helping-your-child-build-self-confidence

Ten Ways to Help Your Child Solve Problems (Without Lecturing Them). (n.d.). Retrieved from https://www.melbournechildpsychology.com.au/blog/10-ways-to-help-your-child-solve-problems-without-lecturing-them/

Thomas, A. (n.d.). The Secret to Education Excellence: High Expectations. Retrieved from https://thebestschools.org/magazine/high-expectations-educations-silver-bullet/

Tips on Helping Your Child Build Relationships. (n.d.). Retrieved from https://www.zerotothree.org/resources/227-tips-on-helping-your-child-build-relationships

Tips on Helping Your Child Develop Confidence. (2010). Retrieved from https://www.zerotothree.org/resources/226-tips-on-helping-your-child-develop-confidence

Understanding Your Child's Trouble with Social Skills. (n.d.). Retrieved from https://www.understood.org/en/learning-thinking-differences/child-learning-disabilities/social-skills-issues/understanding-childs-trouble-with-social-skills

Vickery, N. (2017). Five Reasons to Encourage Entrepreneurship in Kids. Retrieved from https://www.careermetis.com/reasons-encourage-entrepreneurship-kids/

Villacis, R. (2017). Why Encouraging Entrepreneurship in Your Kids Can Be the Best Investment. Retrieved from https://www.entrepreneur.com/article/292864

Walton, A. (2012). How Parents' Stress Can Hurt a Child, from the Inside Out. Retrieved from https://www.forbes.com/sites/alicegwalton/2012/07/25/how-parents-stress-can-hurt-a-child-from-the-inside-out/#1d60673a6b38

Ward, L. (n.d.). How to Praise Your Kids. Retrieved from https://www.parents.com/toddlers-preschoolers/development/social/how-to-praise-your-kids/

Weiss, R. (2017). Business Ideas for Kids: 30+ Activities to Help Raise Entrepreneurial Kids. Retrieved from https://www.thewaystowealth.com/make-money/business-ideas-for-kids/

Wendt, J. (n.d.). Eight Steps to Help Your Child Learn Problem Solving Skills. Retrieved from https://www.findapsychologist.org/8-steps-to-help-your-child-learn-problem-solving-skills-by-dr-jennifer-wendt/

Why It's Important to Let Your Kid Fail. (2018). Retrieved from https://thriveglobal.com/stories/why-it-s-important-to-let-your-kid-fail/

Why You Should Set High Expectations for Your Children. (n.d.). Retrieved from https://www.triumphantlearning.com/high-expectations/

Woo, M. (2017). How to Get Kids to Do Chores: An Age-by-Age Guide. Retrieved from https://offspring.lifehacker.com/how-to-get-kids-to-do-chores-an-age-by-ag%20e-guide-1819715522

Yoo, S. (2018). Why Letting Your Kids Fail Could Be the Best Thing to Do for Them All Year. Retrieved from https://www.chicagoparent.com/learn/general-parenting/let-your-child-fail/

Ziogas, G. (2018). Encouraging Entrepreneurship in Your Children. Retrieved from https://medium.com/publishous/encouraging-entrepreneurship-in-your-children-4504f076485a

Made in the USA
Middletown, DE
10 February 2020